# Fodor's
# 25 Best

FOD
2015

# MELBOURNE

✚ Map reference to the accompanying fold-out map

⊠ Address

☎ Telephone number

🕔 Opening/closing times

🍴 Restaurant or café

🚆 Nearest rail station

Ⓜ Nearest Metro (subway) station

🚌 Nearest bus route

🛥 Nearest riverboat or ferry stop

♿ Facilities for visitors with disabilities

❓ Other practical information

▷ Further information

ℹ Tourist information

✋ Admission charges: Expensive (over A$25), Moderate (A$15–A$25) and Inexpensive (under A$15)

**This guide is divided into four sections**

• Essential Melbourne: An introduction to the city and tips on making the most of your stay.

• Melbourne by Area: We've broken the city into five areas, and recommended the best sights, shops, entertainment venues, nightlife and restaurants in each one. Suggested walks help you to explore on foot. Farther Afield takes you out of the city.

• Where to Stay: The best hotels, whether you're looking for luxury, budget or something in between.

• Need to Know: The info you need to make your trip run smoothly, including getting about by public transportation, weather tips, emergency phone numbers and useful websites.

**Navigation** In the Melbourne by Area chapter, we've given each area its own color, which is also used on the locator maps throughout the book and the map on the inside front cover.

**Maps** The fold-out map accompanying this book is a comprehensive street plan of Melbourne. The grid on this fold-out map is the same as the grid on the locator maps within the book. We've given grid references within the book for each sight and listing.

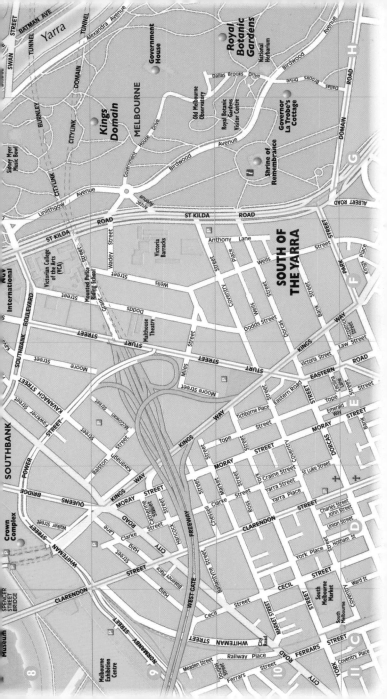

# Contents

**CONTENTS**

# Introducing Melbourne

Melbourne, the capital of the state of Victoria and the heart of the Pacific rim economy, is a lively, forward-looking city, with a modern skyline. Yet the city retains its prosperous Victorian past with its wide boulevards, fine public buildings and infrastructure.

Divided by the quiet waters of the Yarra River, Melbourne is the country's second-largest city after Sydney, with 4.5 million people representing over 180 countries. As the port for rich goldfields in the mid-19th century, Melbourne today exudes a multicultural air, influenced by the descendants of waves of post-World War II European migrants, especially those from Greece and Italy. The city also has a long Chinese heritage and British origins. This combined with latter-day Asian arrivals from Vietnam, India and Sri Lanka, and a new wave of African migrants, makes it one of Australia's most multicultural cities.

Living in the sporting and cultural capital of Australia, Melburnians are as passionate about sport as they are about the arts. The unique Australian Rules Football (AFL) code had its origins here and the city is home to Australia's best collection of art at the two National Gallery of Victoria locations.

For dining and shopping, there is no finer destination in Australia. With thousands of cafés and restaurants serving cuisines from far and wide, food lovers have a great choice, with alfresco dining all the rage. Many of the nation's best wines are produced in Victoria. You will find great shopping within the Central Business District (CBD) and nearby suburbs of Carlton, Fitzroy, South Yarra and Richmond—catering for all tastes and styles.

Only an hour's drive from the city you can see Australia's unique and often shy wildlife. The picturesque Dandenong Ranges on the city's edge are a favored weekend destination, while the Mornington Peninsula is the perfect summer beach escape.

## FACTS AND FIGURES

- The most common language spoken after English is Mandarin (10 percent)
- The oldest building is the Mitre Tavern: 1837
- Residents born overseas: 48 percent
- Of the 18 Australian Football League teams, half are based in Melbourne
- All city center trams in Melbourne are free

## MELBOURNE CUP

On the first Tuesday of November, Australia comes to a standstill, as people are glued to television sets to watch the nation's richest and most prestigious horse race, the Melbourne Cup. Run over 3,200m (2 miles), this handicap race carries prize money in excess of A$6 million. Everyone tries to pick the winner in this notoriously unpredictable race.

## FAMOUS MELBURNIANS

Melbourne is most famous for comedian Barry Humphries, feminist writer Germaine Greer, actor Cate Blanchett and singer Kylie Minogue. The city has produced some of Australia's top sportspeople, too, including aerial skier Alisa Camplin, tennis player Pat Cash and spin bowler Shane Warne.

## GETTING AROUND

The metropolitan region of Melbourne is vast, around 72km (45 miles) north–south and 50km (31 miles) east–west. The well-planned Central Business District (CBD) consists of wide streets in a grid pattern. Since there is often some distance between the important sights, acquaint yourself with the city's trams, which provide a first-rate service, including a free circle route around the CBD. An efficient and comprehensive rail and bus network covers the rest of the city. Melbourne's bike share system is also great for short trips across the city.

# A Short Stay in Melbourne

## DAY 1

**Morning** Have an early breakfast and walk to the **Royal Botanic Gardens** (▷ 60–61) for a quiet stroll around the grounds. You might detour to the nearby **Shrine of Remembrance** (▷ 63), from where you have a fine vista back towards the city.

**Mid-morning** Hop on the St. Kilda Road tram that runs to the city and alight just over the Yarra River at Federation Square. Here you'll find the **Ian Potter Centre: NGV Australia** (▷ 44), the Australian Centre for the Moving Image and nearby park, Birrarung Marr. The city's main tourist information office is also here.

**Lunch** Head along Russell Street to **Chinatown** (▷ 24) for a slice of Asian culture—try one of the many dining options and take a look at the **Chinese Museum** (▷ 24).

**Afternoon** Continue to Spring Street and check out the old **Princess Theatre** (▷ 30) and the **State Parliament House** (▷ 31), the grandiose home to Australia's first government, before arriving at the classic old **Windsor Hotel** (▷ 31), where you can enjoy a sumptuous afternoon tea.

**Dinner** Hop on the City Circle Tram and alight at Flinders Street station. Walk over Princes Bridge to **Southbank** (▷ 62), where you'll find an array of dining options from a range of multicultural cuisines; some restaurants have river and city views.

**Evening** Just nearby, on St. Kilda Road, is **The Arts Centre** (▷ 56), where you can choose a cultural night out from a range of opera, musical and drama performances.

## DAY 2

**Morning** Walk around the CBD and head for the **Laneways** (▷ 25). Be sure to try the chocolate samples at **Koko Black** (▷ 51) and have a coffee break.

**Mid-morning** Walk to the vibrant **Queen Victoria Market** (▷ 27), where you can look for bargain clothing and souvenirs. One section of the market is devoted to food, so you can buy some tasty treats for a picnic lunch.

**Lunch** Take the tram to **St. Kilda** (▷ 97) for a picnic lunch on the seashore. Walk along The Esplanade—there's an arts and crafts market here on Sundays (10am–4pm)—then head to nearby Acland Street's array of tempting pastry shops for a coffee break.

**Afternoon** Return via tram to the city and visit the **Melbourne Aquarium** (▷ 46), one of the city's most popular attractions, where you can see and touch a variety of marine creatures and dive with sharks. Take a tea break at the aquarium's Adventurer's Cafe, then walk back to **Federation Square** (▷ 42–43) to people-watch.

**Dinner** The free City Circle Tram will take you to **NewQuay** (▷ 26) in the Docklands precinct, where you can choose from a wide range of waterside restaurants on NewQuay Promenade. Get on board the **Melbourne Star** (▷ 26) observation wheel for some outstanding views of the city and bay.

**Evening** Walk back into the city for some great nightspots including **James Squire Brewhouse** (▷ 36) for boutique craft beers. Head across to the **Gin Palace** (▷ 36) to finish up in style with a classic martini.

**The Arts Centre ▷ 56** The center of Melbourne's theater, dance, opera and symphonic music.

**Carlton ▷ 82** An art cinema, bookshop, dining and shopping precinct, with an Italian flavor.

**Chinatown ▷ 24** The colorful and vibrant Asian core of the city, with restaurants and food shops.

**City Centre and Laneways ▷ 25** Melbourne's retail heart with stores, boutiques and dining surprises.

**Docklands and Melbourne Star ▷ 26** Waterside area with a giant observation wheel.

**Eureka Skydeck 88 ▷ 57** Catch some amazing 360-degree views of the city and dare to enter The Edge.

**Federation Square ▷ 42–43** The city's meeting place is an architectural icon and cultural draw.

**Fitzroy ▷ 83** The city's most colorful suburb, where hipster rules—quirky bars and funky shops.

**Fitzroy and Treasury Gardens ▷ 72–73** Floral beauty with Captain Cook's Cottage as a centerpiece.

**Heide Museum of Modern Art ▷ 94** Celebrates the work of Australia's early Modernists.

**Ian Potter Centre: NGV Australia ▷ 44** The nation's best collection of Australian art.

**Immigration Museum ▷ 45** All about the city's immigrant communities.

**Melbourne Aquarium ▷ 46–47** See-through tunnels reveal a display of sharks and rays.

**Melbourne Cricket Ground ▷ 74** Australia's most famous sporting arena.

**Melbourne Museum ▷ 84** Learn about the city's past and walk through a living indoor forest.

**Melbourne Zoo ▷ 85** Home to the full range of Australia's fascinating wildlife, plus a world-class gorilla enclosure.

**NGV International ▷ 58–59** Paintings, sculptures and decorative arts of the highest order.

**Old Melbourne Gaol ▷ 28–29** Grim, onetime home to notorious felons and the gallows.

**Queen Victoria Market ▷ 27** Inexpensive clothing, souvenirs and fresh produce are on offer here.

**Rippon Lea House and Como House ▷ 95** Take a look at how the wealthy lived in days gone by.

**Royal Botanic Gardens ▷ 60–61** Stroll among one of the world's great plant collections, then relax on the lawns.

**St. Kilda and Luna Park ▷ 97** Enjoy a trip to the seaside and its classic old fun park.

**Scienceworks ▷ 96** Interactive displays to interest and entertain all ages, plus fantastic shows at the planetarium.

**Southbank and the Crown Complex ▷ 62** Spend some leisure time by the banks of the Yarra River, shopping, dining and more.

**The Yarra River ▷ 48–49** Seeing the city from the river gives a unique perspective.

These pages are a quick guide to the Top 25, which are described in more detail later. Here they are listed alphabetically, and the tinted background shows which area they are in.

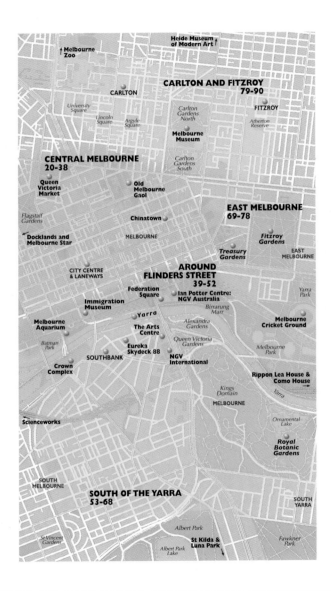

Melbourne Zoo

Heide Museum of Modern Art

CARLTON AND FITZROY
79-90

CARLTON

University Square

Lincoln Square

Argyle Square

FITZROY

Atherton Reserve

Carlton Gardens North

Melbourne Museum

CENTRAL MELBOURNE
20-38

Queen Victoria Market

Old Melbourne Gaol

Carlton Gardens South

EAST MELBOURNE
69-78

Flagstaff Gardens

Chinatown

Docklands and Melbourne Star

MELBOURNE

Fitzroy Gardens

Treasury Gardens

EAST MELBOURNE

CITY CENTRE & LANEWAYS

AROUND FLINDERS STREET
39-52

Federation Square

Ian Potter Centre: NGV Australia

Yarra Park

Immigration Museum

Yarra

Birrarung Marr

Melbourne Aquarium

The Arts Centre

Alexandra Gardens

Melbourne Cricket Ground

Batman Park

Eureka Skydeck 88

Queen Victoria Gardens

Melbourne Park

SOUTHBANK

NGV International

Crown Complex

Kings Domain

Rippon Lea House & Como House

MELBOURNE

Yarra

Scienceworks

Ornamental Lake

Royal Botanic Gardens

SOUTH MELBOURNE

SOUTH OF THE YARRA
53-68

SOUTH YARRA

St Vincent Gardens

Albert Park

Fawkner Park

St Kilda & Luna Park

Albert Park Lake

# Shopping

Melburnians love to shop and the great array of retail outlets, from budget to upper end, attests to this. In fact, the city really is the shopping capital of Australia.

### Australiana
Original Australian design tends to be influenced by nature. Natural materials such as indigenous timbers are used to produce utilitarian bowls and decorative sculptures, regional clays are used in pottery, and wool is often crafted into what could best be described as "wearable art." When it comes to jewelry, Australian opals are much admired and reputable dealers seek to educate potential buyers by displaying rough stones and exhibits explaining how opals are mined. Lustrous South Sea pearls, in all sizes, are great buys, as are gemstones set in Australian gold, and the distinctive pink Argyle diamonds. Check out several shops before settling on a purchase.

### Out and About
Melbourne's retail heart may be the streets and laneways of the CBD (▷ 25), but in a variety of nearby suburbs you'll find interesting specialty shops selling clothing, giftware, souvenirs, books, music and jewelry, plus any number of art galleries. Interesting retail arcades around the city include The Block Arcade, Australia on Collins, Collins Place, Melbourne Central, Melbourne's GPO and the Royal Arcade. Seek out the quirky little stores in the backstreets specializing in handmade jewelry, one-off chic designs, chocolates and unusual gifts.

**BARGAIN SHOPPING**

The post-Christmas season, from late December into January, is bargain shopping time. So is midwinter, in June and July. You can shop for clothing on a budget at any time in department and chain stores. Head to Richmond, where shops selling designer seconds and other well-priced clothes are plentiful. Inner-city suburbs offer bargains in secondhand clothing and many other items.

*From cuddly toys to quirky clothes, Aboriginal objects to handmade hats—shopping Melbourne style*

International brand names are available from the big retail stores Myer and David Jones, as well as from shops at the upper end of Collins Street and in South Yarra and Toorak. Be sure to trawl colorful Brunswick Street in Fitzroy for hipster fashions and funky homeware, second-hand goods, books and alternative art.

### Head for a Bargain

For discount retailing, start at the Queen Victoria Market, but check out the Spencer Outlet Centre (▷ 35) in Spencer Street. Bridge Road and Swan Street in Richmond offer designer seconds and well-priced clothes are plentiful. Be sure to check out the Sunday arts and crafts markets at the Arts Centre and St. Kilda, and the Saturday book market at Federation Square. The Prahran Market (▷ 66) has fresh fruit and vegetables, and deli goods including organic produce. High Street in Armadale has many antique dealers and art galleries. If you have some extra time, make the trip to the nearby attractive town of Daylesford, where one of Victoria's largest outdoor markets is held at the old railway station.

### Shopping Hours

Shops in the city and in designated shopping areas are generally open 10–6 on Monday to Thursday and Saturday to Sunday, and 10–9 on Friday. Individual hours do vary, so call ahead or check their website, especially at weekends.

### BOOKS ON AUSTRALIA

To find out what the city was like in the 19th century, read *The Rise and Fall of Marvellous Melbourne* by Graeme Davidson. To learn about the original inhabitants, read *Aboriginal Australians* by Richard Broome. Tim Flannery's *The Future Eaters* is a fascinating ecological history of Australia. For a look at the origins of Melbourne as the gateway to the Victorian goldfields, read Volume 3 of Manning Clark's *A History of Australia*. For first settlement encounters between Europeans and Aborigines, read Inga Clendinnen's *Dancing With Strangers*.

# Shopping by Theme

Whether you're looking for a department store, a quirky boutique, or something in between, you'll find it all in Melbourne. On this page shops are listed by theme. For a more detailed write-up, see the individual listings in Melbourne by Area.

**Australiana**
Kirra Galleries (▷ 65)
Koorie Connections (▷ 35)
R. M. Williams (▷ 35)
South Yarra Arthouse (▷ 66)

**Books and Music**
ABC Shop (▷ 34)
The Book Grocer (▷ 34)
Brunswick Street Bookstore (▷ 88)
City Basement Books (▷ 51)
Greville Records (▷ 65)
Hill of Content (▷ 34)
Kay Craddock (▷ 35)
Mary Martin Bookshop (▷ 65)
Music Swop Shop (▷ 88)
Polyester (▷ 88)
Readings (▷ 88)
Syber's Books (▷ 66)

**Fashion**
Alpha60 (▷ 88)
Dakota 501 (▷ 65)
Denim Deluxe (▷ 88)
Le Louvre (▷ 65)
Quick Brown Fox (▷ 88)
Retrostar Vintage Clothing (▷ 51)
Saks (▷ 66)
Tomorrow Never Knows (▷ 88)
Uniqlo (▷ 35)

**Food and Drink**
A1 Lebanese Bakery (▷ 103)
Adriano Zumbo (▷ 65)
David Jones Food Hall (▷ 34)
De Bortoli Winery and Restaurant (▷ 103)
Haigh's Chocolates (▷ 65)
Koko Black (▷ 51)
The Original Lolly Store (▷ 88)
Phillippa's Bakery Provisions (▷ 103)
Richmond Hill Café and Larder (▷ 77)

**Jewelry and Gems**
Aqua J (▷ 65)
Ashley Opals (▷ 34)
Ian Sharp (▷ 65)
Keshett (▷ 35)
Palm Beads (▷ 66)
Rutherford Antiques (▷ 35)

**Markets**
Armadale Antique Centre (▷ 103)
Camberwell Sunday Market (▷ 103)
Campbellfield Trash and Treasure Market (▷ 103)
Greville Village Market (▷ 65)
Prahran Market (▷ 66)
Queen Victoria Market (▷ 27, panel 34)
Rose Street Artists' Market (▷ 88)
St. Kilda Esplanade Market (▷ 103)
South Melbourne Market (▷ 66)
The Sunday Art Market (▷ 66)

**Shopping Areas**
Carlton (▷ 88)
Fitzroy (▷ 88)
Richmond (▷ 77)
St. Kilda (▷ 103)
Southgate (▷ 66)
South Yarra & Prahran (▷ 66)
Williamstown (▷ 103)

**Shopping Centers**
The Block Arcade (▷ 34)
Bonds Outlet (▷ 77)
Collins Place (▷ 34)
Collins Street ("Paris End") (▷ 34)
David Jones (▷ 34)
The Galleria (▷ 34)
Jam Factory (▷ 65)
Melbourne Central (▷ 35)
Myer (▷ 35)
Royal Arcade (▷ 35)
St. Collins Lane (▷ 35)
Spencer Outlet Centre (▷ 35)

**Specialist Shops**
Australian Geographic Shop (▷ 34)
City Hatters (▷ 51)
Dinosaur Designs (▷ 65)
Downies Coins (▷ 65)
Ishka Handcrafts (▷ 88)
Make Designed Objects (▷ 88)
Matchbox (▷ 103)
National Wool Museum Shop (▷ 103)
Ozmosis (▷ 35)
Signed and Numbered (▷ 66)
Third Wing (▷ 66)
Vintage Sole (▷ 66)

# Melbourne by Night

Melbourne's diverse nightlife has something for everyone—from the high arts of opera, classical music and cutting-edge drama to a night on the town at a club or pub.

### Cultural Melbourne
The Arts Centre (▷ 56) presents excellent opera, ballet and classical music performances. The orchestra performs at Hamer Hall, the State Theatre hosts opera, and the center's Playhouse presents a variety of theatrical productions. Classical music concerts are also given at the Melbourne Town Hall, the Conservatorium of Music and the Sidney Myer Music Bowl. Lavish musicals can be enjoyed in Melbourne's fabulous old theaters, such as The Princess and Her Majesty's, while the Last Laugh Comedy Club (▷ 36) has a dinner show with professional stand-up acts on Friday and Saturday nights.

### Out on the Town
For that special night out you'll find national and international stars performing at the Crown Entertainment Complex (▷ 62), Rod Laver Arena (▷ 75), The Forum (▷ 51) and the Melbourne Recital Centre (▷ 67). Melbourne has a vibrant gay and lesbian scene, especially in St. Kilda, South Yarra and Collingwood. Check out samesame.com.au/whatson/melbourne for a comprehensive guide of gay and lesbian events in the city. Every Friday, *The Age* newspaper publishes *EG*, an entertainment guide that lists the various options around the city and the suburbs. Only Melbourne (onlymelbourne.com.au) is another good source of information.

**Dazzling scenes of Melbourne illuminated at night**

### GETTING HOME LATE AT NIGHT
While trams stop running at 11pm from Sunday to Thursday, this is extended to 1am on Friday and Saturday nights. The Nightrider bus service operates between 12.30am and 4.30am on Saturday and Sunday mornings and suburban trains run to 1am. Buy a myki card to use on all public transport.

# Eating Out

People from more than 180 nations make Melbourne their home, so there may be some truth in the maxim that you can eat your way around the world here. The city has thousands of restaurants, most offering a range of Victoria's fine wines.

### Home Talent

Australian chefs have made a name for themselves worldwide and Modern Australian, which fuses European and Asian food styles with local ingredients, has arrived as a distinct cutting-edge cuisine. Dishes incorporating Aboriginal foods containing bush tucker ingredients have their own unique flavor. There are plenty of Greek and Italian restaurants, and, not surprisingly, seafood is popular in this bayside city. Local specialties include Melbourne rock oysters, kingfish, huge prawns, Tasmanian scallops and South Australian tuna. Appropriately, many seafood restaurants have waterfront locations, where you can buy excellent fish and chips to take away—St. Kilda, NewQuay and Williamstown are great spots for alfresco dining.

### Melbourne's Asian Restaurants

The city's best Chinese cuisine is at the pinnacle of quality, along with refined cuisine from Japan, India, Indonesia, Burma, Taiwan, Korea, Laos and other Asian countries. Most Asian restaurants are reasonably priced and many are BYO—bring your own alcohol. The best Thai restaurants are equal to those found anywhere outside Thailand. Thai dishes are light and tasty—made with fresh produce and delicate spices and herbs. Vietnamese cuisine rivals Thai cuisine in popularity.

**HOME GROWN**

Victoria has a strong rural industry supplying prime beef and lamb, all types of seafood, and fresh fruit and vegetables. And dairy produce, in the form of specialty cheeses and yoghurts, is particularly worth seeking out. Restaurants draw on this produce for their ingredients.

*Dining alfresco is a popular pastime for Melburnians and visitors alike*

# Restaurants by Cuisine

There are restaurants to suit all tastes and budgets in Melbourne. On this page they are listed by cuisine. For a more detailed description of each restaurant, see Melbourne by Area.

## Asian
Blue Chillies (▷ 90)
Bokchoy Tang (▷ 52)
Burmese House (▷ 78)
Chine on Paramount (▷ 37)
Flower Drum (▷ 38)
Hwaro Korean BBQ (▷ 38)
Kenzan (▷ 52)
Kunis (▷ 38)
Orita's (▷ 68)
Saké Restaurant (▷ 68)
Warung Agus (▷ 38)

## Cafés
Cucina e Bar (▷ 37)
Blue Train Café (▷ 52)
Café Chinotto (▷ 52)
The Commune (▷ 78)
The Deck (▷ 68)
George Street Café (▷ 78)
The Pavilion (▷ 78)
Pellegrini's Espresso Bar (▷ 38)
University Café (▷ 90)

## Contemporary
Arintji (▷ 52)
Becco (▷ 37)
Circa (▷ 106)
Coda Bar & Restaurant (▷ 52)
Cumulus Inc (▷ 52)
Donovans (▷ 106)
Fenix (▷ 78)
The Groove Train (▷ 68)
Hairy Canary (▷ 38)
Jimmy Watson's Wine Bar & Restaurant (▷ 90)
Movida Aqui (▷ 38)
The Point (▷ 68)
Pure South (▷ 68)
Richmond Hill Café & Larder (▷ 78)
Sapore (▷ 106)
Vegie Bar (▷ 90)

## European
Bar Lourinha (▷ 37)
Caffè e Cucina (▷ 68)
City Wine Shop (▷ 37)
D.O.C. (▷ 90)
European (▷ 37)
France Soir (▷ 68)
Grossi Florentino (▷ 38)
Hofbrauhaus (▷ 38)
Noir (▷ 78)
Pireaus Blues (▷ 90)
Radii (▷ 78)
Spitiko (▷ 68)
Tsindos (▷ 38)

## Out of Town
The Healesville Hotel (▷ 106)
Portsea Hotel (▷ 106)
Sky High Restaurant (▷ 106)
Vue Grand Hotel (▷ 106)
Wild Oak Café (▷ 106)

## Seafood
Harry's Kiosk (▷ 106)
Hooked Fitzroy (▷ 90)
Sails on the Bay (▷ 106)

## Thai/Vietnamese
Lemongrass (▷ 90)
Minh Tan II (▷ 78)
Seheri (▷ 68)
Thai Thani (▷ 90)
Viet Rose (▷ 90)

# Top Tips For...

These great suggestions will help you tailor your ideal visit to Melbourne, no matter how you choose to spend your time. Each sight or listing has a fuller write-up elsewhere in the book.

### SAMPLING LOCAL CUISINE

**Classic Italian dishes** are prepared using only the best produce at D.O.C. (▷ 90).
**Melbourne's finest Cantonese cuisine** can be sampled at the elegant Flower Drum (▷ 38) in Chinatown.

### OUTDOOR DINING

**Fancy breakfast outside**—then try The Pavilion (▷ 78) in Fitzroy Gardens with its tasty café-style fare.
**The free City Circle Tram** will take you to NewQuay (▷ 26) in the Docklands precinct, where you can choose from a range of waterside restaurants.

*Pasta and black truffle sauce (top); flowers in Fitzroy Gardens (above)*

### SPECTATOR SPORTS

**Catch an Aussie Rules football game** at the Melbourne Cricket Ground (▷ 74).
**Rod Laver Arena** (▷ 75) is the home of tennis. If you are in the city while it's taking place, get tickets to the Australian Open for a day.

### FREE THINGS

**At the Royal Botanic Gardens** (▷ 60–61) you can stroll among one of the world's great plant collections or take in an open-air performance.
**See some of the world's most admired** paintings, sculptures and decorative arts at the NGV International (▷ 58–59).

*Rod Laver Arena (above right); plenty of space for displaying the NGV International's superb art collection (right)*

*cal culture meets
odern lifestyle
elow)*

### LEARNING ABOUT LOCAL CULTURE

**The nation's best collection of Australian art,** with many Impressionist icons, can be found in the Ian Potter Centre (▷ 44) at Federation Square. **Koorie Connections** (▷ 35) features works by contemporary Aboriginal artists, plus crafts, including the ubiquitous boomerang.

### GOING OUT ON THE TOWN

**Head to Chloe's Bar** at Young and Jacksons (▷ 51) to admire the famous nude portrait and Melbourne icon, and to enjoy a craft beer or cider. **James Squire Brewhouse** at the Portland Hotel (▷ 36) serves James Squire beers and also offers an extensive range of cocktails.

### STAYING AT BUDGET HOTELS

**At the Space Hotel** (▷ 109) rooms cost around A$100 per night and there's a rooftop sundeck with a spa.
**Near the Princess Theatre** is the City Limits hotel (▷ 109), conveniently located in the heart of the Melbourne CBD.

*Backpackers on a budget
(above)*

### ENTERTAINING THE KIDS

**Scienceworks** (▷ 96) is fun, with lots of hands-on exhibits. Don't miss the Lightning Room.
**The Fire Services Museum** (▷ 75) has a display of firefighting memorabilia and a collection of restored fire trucks.

*The Planetarium at the
Scienceworks museum (left)*

*Melbourne leisure—out on the town or out in the woods (below)*

## A GIRLS' NIGHT OUT

**Try one of Melbourne's favorite pubs,** the Transport Hotel (▷ 51) at Federation Square, with live music and DJs every night of the week.
**Book in to see a show** at La Mama Theatre (▷ 89), then wander onto Lygon Street for an after-theater drink.

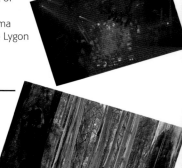

## A WALK ON THE WILD SIDE

**Phillip Island** (▷ 101) has a substantial waterbird population and there are elevated boardwalks through bushland for easy viewing. Be sure not to miss the nesting penguins.
**The scenic Dandenong Ranges** (▷ 99) are less than an hour's drive from the CBD, and have lots of mountain forest walking trails.

## CUTTING-EDGE ARCHITECTURE

**Going green**—The 10-story university building, RMIT Design Hub (▷ 30–31), incorporates all aspects of sustainability in its all-embracing eco design.
**The Eureka Skydeck 88** (▷ 57) is the observation deck at the top of the Eureka Tower and offers panoramic viewing of Melbourne and surrounds.

*The striking Eureka Tower (above)*

## BIRDS AND ANIMALS

**One of Australia's top wildlife parks** is Healesville Sanctuary (▷ 99), set in the foothills of the scenic Yarra Valley.
**Home to the full range** of Australia's wildlife, Melbourne Zoo (▷ 85) also has a world-class gorilla enclosure, set in a rain forest.

*A lowland gorilla having fun at the excellent Melbourne Zoo (right)*

# Melbourne by Area

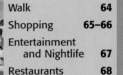

# Central Melbourne

Central Melbourne, the shopping and dining epicenter of the city, has been revitalized by an influx of residents and waterside development in the Docklands district.

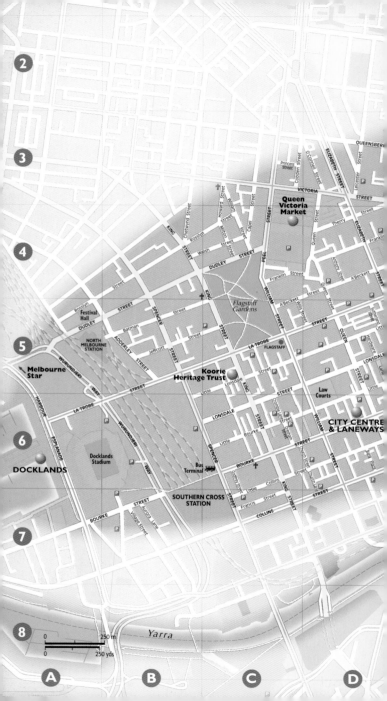

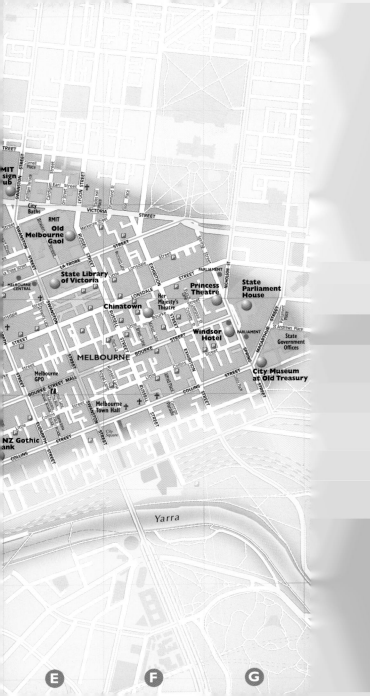

# Chinatown

TOP
25

*The streets behind the stone lions, where the city's Chinatown comes alive on carnival day*

## THE BASICS

chinatownmelbourne.com.au

➕ F5

✉ Little Bourke Street (east)

🍴 Many restaurants

🚇 Parliament

🚋 City Circle Tram

**Chinese Museum**

chinesemuseum.com.au

➕ F5

✉ 22 Cohen Place

☎ 9662 2888

🕐 Daily 10–5

🚇 Parliament

🚋 City Circle Tram

♿ Moderate

💲 Inexpensive

❓ Guided/audiovisual tours

## HIGHLIGHTS

● Interesting shops; restaurants
● Chinese Museum—book ahead for the Chinatown Heritage walk (minimum six people)
● Distinctive architecture

**The Chinese community has been settled in bustling Little Bourke Street since the gold-rush days of the 1850s. Today, excellent restaurants and specialist shops sit next to herbalists and small shops selling Chinese goods and food.**

**The backstreets** Chinese gates and two stone lions mark this distinctive part of Little Bourke Street, between Exhibition and Swanston streets, although it spills over into the adjoining streets and lanes. After the gold rush, many Chinese immigrants opened shops, furniture factories and other businesses here, and some of the 19th-century Victorian buildings commissioned by Chinese businessmen and designed by notable architects of the day still stand. Today, Asian supermarkets, restaurants and cake shops cater for Chinese tastes.

**Chinese Museum** In this museum in Cohen Place, off Little Bourke Street, there are excellent photographic exhibits on the history and culture of the Chinese people in Australia, together with an interesting walk-through re-creation of the experience of the Chinese on the gold fields in early Victoria. Among the exhibits is a life-size replica of a Warrior General from the second century BC, the only such replica outside China, and the Millennium Dragon, reputedly the world's largest processional dragon that is paraded through the streets each year at the Moomba Festival in March, a 10-day carnival with cultural and sporting events.

*Just relaxing or taking a boat down the river, there's plenty to do in central Melbourne*

**CENTRAL MELBOURNE** TOP 25

**Compact and easy to explore, the center of Melbourne is set out in a rectangular grid. When you get tired of walking, just jump on a tram—all trams are free in the city center Free Tram Zone.**

**City Centre** Focusing on the Central Business District or CBD, you will find most of the main department stores, hotels, offices and banks, as well as the fine old Victorian churches, theaters and public institutions that give Melbourne its personality in this central area. Excellent restaurants and cafés are scattered throughout the city center. Within walking distance, across the Yarra River to the south, are parks and gardens, The Arts Centre and National Gallery of Victoria, the Southgate shopping and dining complex on Southbank, and Crown Casino. The best way to get a sense of the place is on foot, with occasional rides on the free City Circle Tram.

**Melbourne's meeting place** On the edge of the CBD, Federation Square (▷ 42–43) is the size of a city block. The excellent visitor center here will provide help with your travel plans.

**Shopping** Melbourne has great shopping opportunities. The retail area is bounded roughly by Elizabeth, Collins, Spring and La Trobe streets. Check out the city's lanes and arcades, especially the Royal and Block Arcades. Look for Hardware Lane, a stretch of old warehouses between Bourke and Lonsdale streets, converted into restaurants, bars and shops.

---

### THE BASICS

thatsmelbourne.com.au

🚩 D6

✉ Melbourne Visitor Information Centre, Federation Square, corner of Swanston and Flinders streets

☎ 9658 9658

🕐 Daily 9–6

🍴 Many cafés, restaurants and shops

🚃 City Circle Tram

♿ Varies

❓ Shopping hours may vary, but city shops are generally open Mon–Thu 10–6, Fri 10–9, Sat–Sun 10–5
Be sure to book a Hidden Secrets Tour: ☎ 9663 3358, hiddensecretstours. com

---

### HIGHLIGHTS

- Federation Square
- Lanes and arcades
- Specialist shops
- Historic buildings

# Docklands and Melbourne Star

TOP 25

*The NewQuay area has some striking modern sculpture*

## THE BASICS

thatsmelbourne.com.au
waterfrontcity.com.au
melbournestar.com

➕ A6

✉ Harbour Esplanade, Docklands

☎ 9658 9658

🕐 Daily until late

🍴 Many fine restaurants

🚋 City Circle Tram; also city trams 48, 70, 86

♿ Good

🎟 Free

## HIGHLIGHTS

● NewQuay
● Waterfront City entertainment and leisure development
● Water views
● Melbourne Star observation wheel
● Dining precinct

**Just minutes away from Melbourne's CBD, Docklands is the city's waterfront area, with restaurants, galleries, shops and leisure activities set alongside the Yarra River and Victoria Harbour.**

**Docklands** About the same size as the Melbourne CBD, Docklands has marinas, promenades, parklands, restaurants and residential areas connected to the city by excellent public transport, scenic walkways and cycling lanes.

**NewQuay** NewQuay, at the northwestern edge of the harbor, has many restaurants offering a wide range of cuisines, cafés, bars and fashionable stores—all situated along the promenade, with stunning harbor and city views. Waterfront City is a vibrant mix of dining, retail, entertainment, residential and commercial elements. Many seasonal events take place in the public Piazza, which can hold up to 10,000 people.

**Melbourne Star** The 120m (394-foot) observation wheel has 360-degree views as far as the Dandenong Ranges. The 21 air-conditioned cabins carry 20 people on a half-hour ride. There's an in-cabin audio tour in English.

**Over the water** Webb Bridge provides a pedestrian and cycle crossing to residential Yarra's Edge. Here you'll find excellent restaurants and a place for a quiet stroll along the riverfront promenade.

# Queen Victoria Market

*The array of mouth-watering produce on sale at the bustling Queen Victoria Market*

**Some of the original buildings still stand at Australia's biggest and most popular outdoor market, which offers just about everything from food and footwear to plants, art and souvenirs.**

**History** Just a few minutes' walk from the city center, this bustling, chaotic retail complex is the city's largest market, with over a thousand stalls on 7ha (17 acres). The complex is the last of several city markets. Many of the present buildings date back to the 19th century, including the Meat Hall (1869), Sheds A to F (1878) and the two-story shops on Victoria Street (1887).

**Markets** The colorful traders are an attraction in their own right, promoting their wares and bantering with passersby. In the Lower Market are the Meat Hall, with meat, fish and game; the Dairy Hall, with delicatessens and bakeries; and a section with fresh fruit and vegetables, as well as a huge range of ready-to-eat foods. On a nearby rise, a stretch of open-sided sheds, known as the Upper Market, houses a wide variety of fresh produce, clothing and souvenirs. From Friday to Sunday, a wine market operates.

**Guided tours** The Foodies Dream Tour provides a chance to taste Australian cheeses, nuts, preserves, meats and exotic tropical fruits, while the Heritage Market Tour takes you through the market's original buildings and describes a century of its fascinating past. Note that the Heritage Tour is for groups only.

## THE BASICS

qvm.com.au

✚ C4

✉ Corner of Elizabeth and Victoria streets

☎ Information: 9320 5822. Tours: 9320 5835

🕐 Tue, Thu 6–2, Fri 5am–6pm, Sat 6–3, Sun 9–4

🍴 Many cafés and restaurants nearby and plenty of stalls selling snack food and coffee

Ⓜ Melbourne Central

🚋 Any tram on Elizabeth Street northbound to stop 7

♿ Moderate

## HIGHLIGHTS

● The stallholders
● Stalls selling exotic tropical fruits and Australian cheeses
● Historic buildings
● Market tours
● Weekend Wine Market

# Old Melbourne Gaol

**TOP 25**

*Ned Kelly's death mask (middle) on display at the notorious Old Melbourne Gaol*

## THE BASICS

oldmelbournegaol.com.au
➕ E4
✉ 377 Russell Street
☎ 9663 7228
🕐 Daily 9.30–5
🚋 City Circle Tram
♿ Limited
💰 Moderate
❓ Tour groups by arrangement. "Such a Life," a fascinating look at Ned Kelly's life and legend, is performed every Sat at 12.30 and 2

## HIGHLIGHTS

● Bluestone building
● Death masks
● Ned Kelly memorabilia
● Candlelight Night Tours
● Prisoners' Stories

**This historic bluestone prison is fixed in national folklore as the place where Australia's most famous bushranger, Ned Kelly, was hanged. Here you can see the gallows and several death masks.**

**A gruesome past** This grim, gloomy place, with thick walls, small cells and heavy iron doors, is Victoria's oldest surviving penal establishment. To spend some time within its walls is to begin to understand the realities of prison life in the 19th century. Begun in 1841 and completed in 1864, it was designed along the lines of the Pentonville Modern Prison in London and consists of three levels of cells. The gallows, where 135 men and women were hanged, is the centerpiece of the complex. The death masks of some of those executed are on display, along with their stories. The most famous hanging was that of the bushranger Ned Kelly, one of the nation's folk heroes, an outlaw executed in 1880, whose famous last words were, "Such is life." A wooden tableau depicts the Kelly execution and nightly performances re-create the prison's gruesome past. The present cell block was in use until 1929 when the last prisoners were transferred to other prisons.

**In the cells** The penal museum presents displays and provides information on many infamous inmates, displays the Hangman's Box with its original contents and chronicles incarcerations. The flogging frame is on view along with the punishment instruments.

# More to See

### ANZ GOTHIC BANK
This highly decorated Gothic revival bank, completed in 1887, has been compared to the Doge's Palace in Venice. Its magnificent interior, with gold leaf ornamentation amid graceful arches and pillars, features decorative shields from the countries and cities that the original bank, the England, Scottish and Australian Bank, traded with.
✚ D6 ✉ 386 Collins Street ☎ 9273 5555 🕐 Mon–Fri 10–3 🚋 City Circle Tram ✋ Free

### CITY MUSEUM AT OLD TREASURY
oldtreasurybuilding.org.au
This superb example of neoclassical architecture, one the city's finest buildings, was built between 1858 and 1862 as the repository for the young colony's gold reserves. Now a museum, it showcases the wealth of the gold-rush era.
✚ G5 ✉ 30 Spring Street ☎ 9651 2233 🕐 Sun–Fri 10–4 🚋 City Circle Tram ✋ Inexpensive

### KOORIE HERITAGE TRUST
koorieheritagetrust.com
The trust's Cultural Centre features works by contemporary Aboriginal artists, plus a permanent exhibition that includes traditional artifacts and rare books. Its oral history unit offers a fascinating insight into the rich history and culture of Australia's southeastern indigenous people.
✚ C5 ✉ 295 King Street ☎ 8622 2600 🕐 Mon–Fri 10–5 🚋 City Circle Tram to La Trobe and King streets ✋ Free

### PRINCESS THEATRE
marrinergroup.com.au/theatreprincess
One of the world's grand old theaters, The Princess was built in 1854. Today it mounts major musical productions.
✚ G5 ✉ 163 Spring Street ☎ 9299 9800 🕐 Daily 🍴 Bistro 🚋 City Circle Tram ✋ Free

### RMIT DESIGN HUB
designhub.rmit.edu.au
This visionary design hub is a soaring 10-story building covered

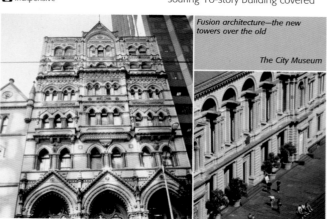

Fusion architecture—the new towers over the old

The City Museum

in circles of sandblasted glass that move with the sun and wind, helping to moderate the temperature of the building. The five-star energy building has a number of exhibition spaces that are open to the public.
🚹 E3 ✉ Corner of Victoria and Swanston streets ☎ 9925 2260 🕐 Tue–Fri 11–6, Sat 12–5 🚋 City Circle Tram ✋ Free

### STATE LIBRARY OF VICTORIA
slv.vic.gov.au
This large library complex, with an impressive domed reading room, is an attraction in its own right. There are changing exhibitions and a vast collection of books that can be browsed through on request.
🚹 E4 ✉ 328 Swanston Street ☎ 8664 7002 🕐 Mon–Thu 10–9, Fri–Sun 10–6. Closed public hols 🚋 City Circle Tram ✋ Free

### STATE PARLIAMENT HOUSE
parliament.vic.gov.au
Built during the gold rush in 1856, and amended with a wide flight of bluestone steps and towering Doric columns in 1892, this grand building was the first home of the Australian Parliament, until it moved to Canberra in 1927. You can attend a session when the State Parliament is sitting, and there are daily tours.
🚹 G5 ✉ Spring Street ☎ 9651 8911 🕐 Tours: Mon–Fri 9.30–4 🚋 City Circle Tram ✋ Free

### WINDSOR HOTEL
thehotelwindsor.com.au
A Melbourne landmark listed by the National Trust and the grandest hotel in Australia, the meticulously restored Windsor has all the elegance of a luxury 19th-century hotel. Even if you don't stay here, pop in to admire the sweeping, wrought-iron staircase, the ornately detailed foyer and the rich detail of the Grand Ballroom. The hotel is in Spring Street, just opposite the State Parliament House.
🚹 G5 ✉ 111 Spring Street ☎ 9633 6000 🕐 24-hour reception 🚋 City Circle Tram ✋ Free for a look

*A good meeting place—the entrance to the State Parliament House*

# City Heritage Walk

Learn about Melbourne's fascinating past on this walk through the city's heritage precincts, streets, arcades and laneways.

**DISTANCE:** 4km (2.5 miles)  **ALLOW:** 3 hours

**START**

**IMMIGRATION MUSEUM**
(▷ 45)
🞥 D7  🚋 City Circle Tram

**1** Begin at the Immigration Museum and head for King Street, via Willliam Street and Flinders Lane. Look for the bluestone buildings along the way, before turning into Collins Street.

**2** On Collins Street, right next to the Rialto Towers, check out the old Rialto Hotel and the nearby ornate 19th-century office buildings.

**3** Detour along William Street to Little Collins and back to Collins via Bank Place. You will pass the grand old Australian Club (William Street), Stalbridge Chambers (Little Collins Street) and the Mitre Tavern (Bank Place).

**4** Back in Collins Street, view the ornate banking chamber of the ANZ Gothic Bank (▷ 30) and below it the Banking Museum.

**END**

**WINDSOR HOTEL** (▷ 31)
🞥 G5  🚋 City Circle Tram

**8** In Spring Street, visit the City Museum at Old Treasury (▷ 30), the State Parliament House (▷ opposite and 31) and the splendid Windsor Hotel.

**7** After inspecting the grand old Melbourne Town Hall, proceed down Collins Street towards Spring Street to see its three blocks of fine churches, theaters, stores and the exclusive Melbourne Club.

**6** Turn into Howey Place; walk to Capitol Arcade, past the art deco Capitol Theatre, into Swanston Street, and back into Collins Street.

**5** Just past Elizabeth Street, look for the entrance to The Block Arcade and follow this covered shopping area through to the Royal Arcade in Little Collins Street.

# Shopping

### ABC SHOP
shop.abc.net.au
Operated by the Australian Broadcasting Corporation, this interesting shop sells books, videos, music and audio cassettes, CDs, toys and clothes relating to Australian TV and radio programs.
🔢 E5 ✉ 269 Lonsdale Street ☎ 9639 0564 🚋 City Circle Tram

### ASHLEY OPALS
ashleyopals.com.au
Jewelry made from an exclusive range of opal stones, pearls, diamonds and precious gems.
🔢 F6 ✉ 85 Collins Street ☎ 9654 4866 🚋 City Circle Tram

### AUSTRALIAN GEOGRAPHIC SHOP
shop.australiangeographic. com.au
Australia's best artists, writers, photographers, craftspeople and designers join forces to produce clothing, prints, stationery, birdhouses, telescopes and more.
🔢 E5 ✉ 287 Lonsdale Street ☎ 8616 6726 🚋 City Circle Tram

### THE BLOCK ARCADE
theblockarcade.com.au
Opened in 1892, this National Trust-classified arcade has an intricately tiled floor, decorative ironwork, stained-glass windows and over 30 shops on three levels.
🔢 E6 ✉ 282 Collins Street ☎ 9654 5244 🚋 City Circle Tram

### THE BOOK GROCER
bookgrocer.libro.com.au
This Australian, family-owned bookseller stocks a large range of discounted books.
🔢 D6 ✉ 464 Collins Street ☎ 9620 0990 🚋 City Circle Tram

### COLLINS PLACE
collinsplace.com.au
This large, stylish and popular shopping center, in the heart of Collins Street, has many specialist shops.
🔢 G5 ✉ 45 Collins Street ☎ 9655 3600 🚋 City Circle Tram

---

## DELICACIES

To get an idea of the best Australian produce, be sure to visit the Queen Victoria Market (▷ 27), where you can sample cheeses, meats and exotic fruits. Look for cheese from the Yarra Valley and Tasmania, and seafood from the cooler southern oceans—everything from scallops to Tasmanian smoked salmon (specialist fishmongers will cook your selection). Fruits grown in Victoria include strawberries, pears and apples. Vegetables such as snow peas, asparagus and broccoli are plentiful, as well as the only native nut to hit the world stage, the macadamia.

---

### COLLINS STREET ("PARIS END")
Many exclusive boutiques are along this elegant stretch of Collins Street, between Swanston and Spring streets.
🔢 G5 ✉ Collins Street 🚋 City Circle Tram

### DAVID JONES
davidjones.com.au
Known to the locals as DJs, this alternative to Myer sells quality goods. Excellent food hall in the Bourke Street shop.
🔢 D6 ✉ Little Bourke, Bourke and Little Collins streets ☎ 9643 2222 🚋 City Circle Tram

### DAVID JONES FOOD HALL
The lower level of this food hall is one of the city's most exclusive food shops.
🔢 D6 ✉ 310 Bourke Street ☎ 9643 2222 🚋 City Circle Tram

### THE GALLERIA
galleria.com.au
Interesting collection of fashion and gift shops.
🔢 E6 ✉ Corner of Elizabeth and Bourke streets ☎ 8611 2992 🚋 City Circle Tram

### HILL OF CONTENT
hillofcontentbookshop.com.au
This bookshop has a solid range of current titles, with some specials and an excellent selection of cookbooks.
🔢 F5 ✉ 86 Bourke Street ☎ 9662 9472 🚋 Tram 86, 96

### KAY CRADDOCK

kaycraddock.com
One of Melbourne's top secondhand and rare books dealers.
⊞ E6 ✉ 156 Collins Street ☎ 9654 8506 ⦿ Mon–Fri 10–6, Sat 10–4 🚃 City Circle Tram

### KESHETT

keshett.com.au
Contemporary and antique jewelry from the art deco, Edwardian, art nouveau and Victorian eras.
⊞ E6 ✉ 323 Collins Street ☎ 9654 1514 🚃 City Circle Tram

### KOORIE CONNECTIONS

qvm.com.au/shops-and-stalls/koorie-connections
Authentic Aboriginal arts and crafts gallery owned and operated by Aboriginal people.
⊞ D3 ✉ 145 Victoria Street ☎ 9326 9824 🚃 City Circle Tram

### MELBOURNE CENTRAL

melbournecentral.com.au
This center houses over 290 specialist shops, cafés, restaurants in an original building, once used in the manufacture of gunshot.
⊞ E4 ✉ Corner of Swanston and La Trobe streets ☎ 9922 1100 🚃 City Circle Tram

### MYER

myer.com.au
The biggest department store in the southern

hemisphere sells a wide range of fashion, designer housewares, gifts and cosmetics.
⊞ D6 ✉ Lonsdale, Little Bourke and Bourke streets ☎ 9661 1111 🚃 City Circle Tram

### OZMOSIS

ozmosis.com.au
Everything for the surfer, from boards to beachwear, including the popular Billabong, Rip Curl and Hot Tuna brands.
⊞ E6 ✉ Melbourne Central ☎ 9662 3815 🚃 City Circle Tram

### R. M. WILLIAMS

rmwilliams.com.au
Authentic Australian outback clothing and traditional Aussie footwear.
⊞ E6 ✉ Melbourne Central, 300 Lonsdale Street ☎ 9663 7126 🚃 City Circle Tram

### SHOPPING TOURS

To explore out-of-the-way bargain shopping districts, you might want to call one of the following operators, which organize group shopping tours. Go Get Around (☎ 9579 5771, gogetaroundtours.com.au) specializes in warehouse shopping for clothing and other goods at wholesale prices. Outlet Shopping Tours (☎ 8822 4568, outletshoppingtours.com.au) offers smaller group tours to backstreet wholesalers.

### ROYAL ARCADE

royalarcade.com.au
Australia's oldest retail arcade contains around 30 shops that sell fashion and gifts.
⊞ E6 ✉ 335 Bourke Street Mall 🚃 City Circle Tram

### RUTHERFORD ANTIQUES

rutherford.com.au
Purveys a superb range of fine sterling silver and antique jewelry, from Georgian to art deco.
⊞ E6 ✉ 182 Collins Street ☎ 9650 7878 🚃 City Circle Tram

### ST. COLLINS LANE

stcollinslane.com
Over 65 specialist shops under one roof provide the best in fashion, food and housewares.
⊞ E6 ✉ 260 Collins Street 🚃 City Circle Tram

### SPENCER OUTLET CENTRE

spenceroutletcentre.com.au
More than 100 big-name brands offer discounts of up to 70 percent off fashion and accessories.
⊞ C6 ✉ 1/201 Spencer Street ☎ 8689 7555 🚉 Southern Cross

### UNIQLO

uniqlo.com/au
Head here for popular and innovative Japanese casual wear for men, women and children at affordable prices.
⊞ E5 ✉ 287 Lonsdale Street ☎ 8609 8221 🚃 City Circle Tram

# Entertainment and Nightlife

## BENNETTS LANE JAZZ CLUB

bennettslane.com

One of the best in Melbourne, this small jazz venue attracts top names playing a variety of jazz styles.

✚ F4 ✉ 25 Bennetts Lane ☎ 9663 2856 🕐 Nightly 🚊 City Circle Tram

## CITY BATHS

melbourne.vic.gov.au/ melbournecitybaths

This historic swimming complex is the place to get in a few laps or to just cool off on a hot day. Also has a gym, Jacuzzis, saunas and squash courts.

✚ E4 ✉ 420 Swanston Street ☎ 9663 5888 🕐 Mon–Fri 6am–10pm, Sat–Sun 8–6 🚊 Swanston Street Tram

## COMEDY THEATRE

marrinergroup.com.au/ theatre-comedy

This delightful 1,000-seater theater, modeled on a Florentine palace with a Spanish-style interior, hosts a variety of shows.

✚ F5 ✉ 240 Exhibition Street ☎ 9299 4950 🚊 City Circle Tram

## COOKIE

cookie.net.au

High ceilings, bluestone stairway, balconies overlooking Swanston Street and an incredibly long bar are features of this friendly, spacious establishment.

✚ E5 ✉ 252 Swanston Street ☎ 9663 7660 🕐 Sun–Thu noon–1am, Fri–Sat noon–3am 🚊 City Circle Tram

## THE CROFT INSTITUTE

thecroftinstitute.com

Hidden down an alley, this chemistry lab-cum-brewpub serves experimental house cocktails.

✚ F5 ✉ Croft Alley ☎ 9671 4399 🕐 Mon–Thu 5pm–1am, Fri 5pm–3am, Sat 8pm–3am 🚊 Tram 86, 96

## DOCKLANDS STADIUM

etihadstadium.com.au

This stadium, sponsored by Etihad, hosts a variety of sports, as well as concerts.

✚ A6 ✉ 740 Bourke Street ☎ 8625 7700 🕐 Call for details 🚊 City Circle Tram

### BUYING A TICKET

There are several ways of getting tickets for theater, live music concerts and other events. You can visit the box offices, or purchase online by credit card from ticketing agencies such as Ticketmaster.com.au and Ticketek.com.au. At Half Tix (☎ 9650 9420), a booth in Bourke Street Mall, you can get discounted tickets on the day of performance. At the latter, tickets must be bought in person and paid for in cash (Mon 10–2, Tue–Fri 11–6, Sat 10–4).

## GIN PALACE

ginpalace.com.au

Serious drinkers come here for the classic martinis and the stylish ambience.

✚ E6 ✉ 10 Russell Place ☎ 9654 0533 🕐 Daily 4pm–3am 🚊 City Circle Tram

## HER MAJESTY'S THEATRE

hmt.com.au

This lovely old theater, built in 1866, is one of Melbourne's leading locations for major theatrical productions.

✚ F5 ✉ 219 Exhibition Street ☎ 8643 3300 🚊 City Circle Tram

## JAMES SQUIRE BREWHOUSE

portlandhotel.com.au

The Portland Hotel serves the entire range of James Squire beers, plus cocktails and popular wines.

✚ F5 ✉ 127 Russell Street ☎ 9810 0064 🕐 Noon–late 🚊 City Circle Tram

## LAST LAUGH COMEDY CLUB

thecomedyclub.com.au

Enjoy a dinner show on Friday and Saturday nights, featuring professional local and international stand-up acts.

✚ F6 ✉ Athenaeum Theatre, 188 Collins Street ☎ 9650 1977 🕐 Fri–Sat 7pm–11pm 🚊 11, 12, 39, 109

## MADAME BRUSSELS

madamebrussels.com

This terraced cocktail bar

overlooks the city. A variety of punches are served by staff dressed in tennis whites.

🏛 F5 ✉ 59 Bourke Street
☎ 9662 2775 🕐 Daily noon–1am 🚋 Tram 86, 96

### MELBOURNE TOWN HALL

A major site of choral and orchestral performances, with occasional free concerts.

🏛 E6 ✉ 90–120 Swanston Street ☎ 9658 9658
🚋 City Circle Tram

### PRINCESS THEATRE

marrinergroup.com.au/theatre-princess
Melbourne's most glorious performance space, in one of the city's finest buildings, is home to musicals and other leading theatrical events.

🏛 G5 ✉ 163 Spring Street

☎ 9299 9800 🚋 City Circle Tram

### THE REGENT THEATRE

marrinergroup.com.au/theatre-regent
Opened in 1929 as a picture palace, the Regent is now equipped for stage and screen.

🏛 F6 ✉ 191 Collins Street
☎ 9299 9860 🚋 City Circle Tram

# Restaurants

| PRICES |
| --- |
| Prices are approximate, based on a 3-course meal for one person. |
| $ A$20–A$40 |
| $$ A$41–A$70 |
| $$$ A$71–A$110 |

### BAR LOURINHA ($)

barlourinha.com.au
Casual modern tapas bar. Try the spicy rabbit and olive *empanadillas*.

🏛 F5 ✉ 37 Little Collins Street ☎ 9663 7890
🕐 Mon–Thu noon–11pm, Fri noon–1am, Sat 4pm–1am
🚋 11, 12, 109

### BECCO ($)

becco.com.au
Elegant restaurant with modern Italian fare.

🏛 E6 ✉ 11/25 Crossley Street ☎ 9663 3000
🕐 Lunch and dinner Tue–Sat
🚋 Tram 86, 96

### CHINE ON PARAMOUNT ($$)

chineonparamount.com.au
This is a typical Chinese restaurant where you will find authentic dishes in fine style. Takeout also available.

🏛 F5 ✉ 101 Little Bourke Street ☎ 9663 6556
🕐 Daily 5.30pm–9.30pm
🚋 City Circle Tram

**ASIAN RESTAURANTS**

Chinese restaurants were the main source of Asian cuisine in Melbourne for many years. Now the best of Chinese cuisine has achieved a superb level, and it is being joined by refined cuisine from Indonesia, Myanmar, Taiwan, Korea, Laos and other Asian countries. Most are reasonably priced and many are BYO.

### CITY WINE SHOP ($$)

citywineshop.net.au
You can purchase wine from the shop to enjoy with a quick European-style meal, or choose from a wide range of wines by the glass.

🏛 G4 ✉ 159 Spring Street
☎ 9654 4657 🕐 Breakfast, lunch and dinner daily
🚋 City Circle Tram

### CUCINA E BAR ($)

caterinas.com.au
Enjoy traditional Italian in an intimate basement setting at this popular lunch spot.

🏛 D5 ✉ 221 Queen Street
☎ 9670 8488 🕐 Lunch noon–6 🚋 City Circle Tram

### EUROPEAN ($$$)

theeuropean.com.au
A city favorite, with French and Italian dishes, perfect ambience and great service.

🏠 G4 ✉ 161 Spring Street
☎ 9654 0811 🕐 Breakfast,
lunch and dinner daily
🚋 City Circle Tram

### FLOWER DRUM ($$$)

flower-drum.com
Melbourne's best
Chinese restaurant offers
delicious Cantonese and
other regional food using
seasonal ingredients in
stylish surroundings.
🏠 F5 ✉ 17 Market Lane
☎ 9662 3655 🕐 Daily
10am–11pm 🚋 City Circle
Tram

### GROSSI FLORENTINO ($$$)

grossiflorentino.com
One of Melbourne's
oldest and best restau-
rants, serving traditional
European fare. Elegant
and hard to beat.
🏠 F5 ✉ 80 Bourke Street
☎ 9662 1811 🕐 Daily
7.30am–11.30pm 🚋 City
Circle Tram

### HAIRY CANARY ($$)

This trendy place is noisy
and not for an intimate
dinner for two, but the
modern Mediterranean
fare is inspired.
🏠 E6 ✉ 212 Little Collins
Street ☎ 9654 2471
🕐 Mon–Wed 3pm–3am,
Thu–Fri noon–3am, Sat 9am–
3am, Sun 9am–1am 🚋 City
Circle Tram

### HOFBRAUHAUS ($$)

hofbrauhaus.com.au
Bavarian hospitality, live
music and slap dancing,
and tasty, hearty, tradi-
tional German cuisine.

🏠 G5 ✉ 18–24 Market
Lane ☎ 9663 3361 🕐 Daily
noon–late 🚋 86, 96

### HWARO KOREAN BBQ ($$)

hwaro.com.au
Enjoy authentic Korean
food using high-quality
meats which is cooked
at your table on mini
charcoal barbecues.
🏠 C6 ✉ 562 Little Bourke
Street ☎ 9642 5696
🕐 Sun–Thu 5–10.30pm,
Fri–Sat 5–11pm 🚋 86, 96

### KUNIS ($$)

kunismelbourne.com
This friendly Japanese
restaurant, one of
Melbourne's best, has
a sushi bar as well as a
main dining area.
🏠 G5 ✉ 56 Little Bourke
Street ☎ 9663 7243
🕐 Lunch and dinner daily
🚋 86, 96

---

**EATING OUT**

It has been said that you
can eat your way around
the world in Melbourne,
and with thousands of restaurants, the city may well
be Australia's culinary capital. Immigrants have always
influenced local tastes. In
the past, Europeans set the
standards, but today it is
Asian chefs, more particularly Vietnamese and Thai,
who are affecting what
people eat. Restaurants are
either licensed or BYO—
bring your own alcoholic
beverages.

### MOVIDA AQUI ($$)

movida.com.au
One of five MoVida
restaurants run by
chef Frank Camorra in
Melbourne, this one
serves up exquisite tapas
in an airy terrace restaurant with cityscape views.
🏠 D6 ✉ Level 1, 500
Bourke Street ☎ 9663 3038
🕐 Mon–Fri noon–late, Sat
6pm–late 🚋 86, 96

### PELLEGRINI'S ESPRESSO BAR ($)

A Melbourne institution,
Pellegrini's is a classic
Italian coffee bar offer-
ing excellent espresso
and large helpings of
minestrone, pastas and
salads.
🏠 F5 ✉ 66 Bourke Street
☎ 9662 1885 🕐 Breakfast,
lunch and dinner daily
🚋 Tram 85, 96 ·

### TSINDOS ($$)

tsindosrestaurant.com.au
Tsindos prides itself on its
traditional Greek cuisine
and welcoming family
atmosphere. The menu
includes grilled octopus,
moussaka, lamb on the
spit and seafood.
🏠 E5 ✉ 197 Lonsdale Street
☎ 9663 3194 🕐 Lunch
Mon–Fri, dinner daily 🚋 Any
Swanston Street tram

### WARUNG AGUS ($$)

warungagus.com.au
A long menu of
Indonesian dishes in a
Balinese setting.
🏠 C3 ✉ 305 Victoria Street
☎ 9329 1737 🕐 Dinner
Thu–Sun 🚋 Tram 16

Accessible by the free City Circle Tram, and centered on the dramatic Federation Square, the area around Flinders Street has some of Melbourne's top attractions and pleasant riverside walks.

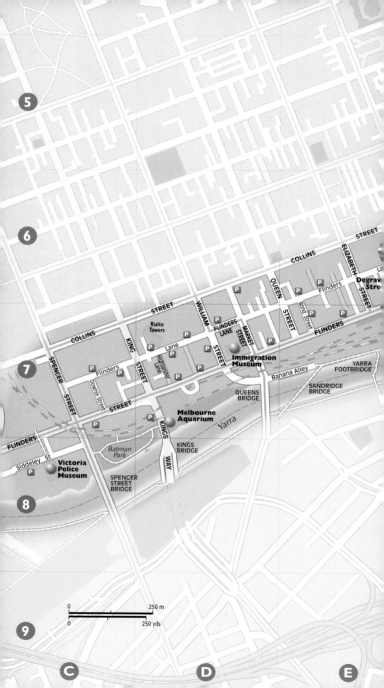

SPRING STREET

EXHIBITION STREET

Lane

Flinders

George Parade

RUSSELL STREET

FLINDERS STREET

Ack La

Regent Theatre

City Square

SWANSTON STREET

Forum Theatre

St Paul's Cathedral

Ian Potter Centre: NGV Australia

RUSSELL ST EXT

Federation Square

BATMAN AVENUE

Birrarung Marr

Flinders Street Station

Princes Walk

Redgum Gully

ST KILDA ROAD

**Yarra**

PRINCES BRIDGE

**F**

**G**

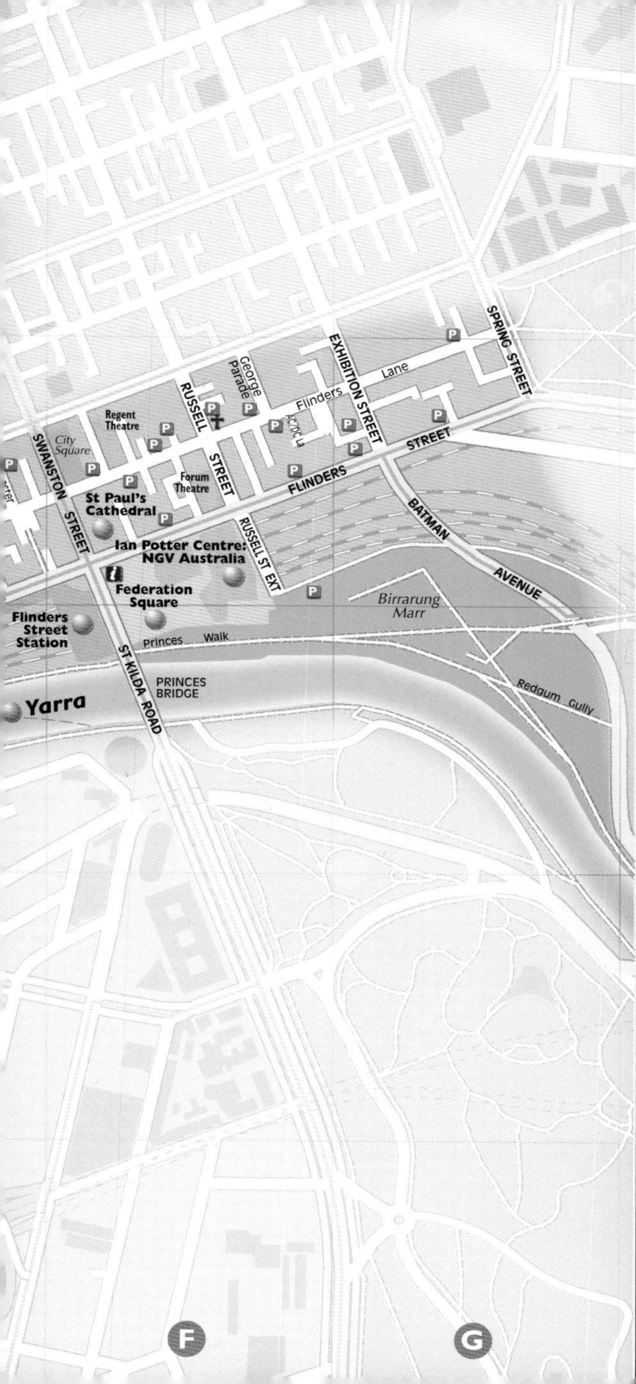

# Federation Square

## HIGHLIGHTS

● Ian Potter Centre: NGV Australia
● Centre for the Moving Image
● Daily guided tours
● Saturday Book Market
● Free concerts at Deakin Edge

## TIP

● Make your first stop the visitor center and ask about the free concerts held here.

**Federation Square, billed as Melbourne's meeting place, has a mix of attractions, including the Ian Potter Centre and the Australian Centre for the Moving Image, along with restaurants, cafés and bars.**

**What's on?** There's usually something interesting happening in this huge complex, which covers a full city block. Built over an old railway yard, Fed Square (as it is known locally) was conceived as a civic heart for the city, and has enough museums, galleries, free attractions and places to dine to keep you busy for at least half a day. The Melbourne Visitor Centre is a must for information on what to see and where to stay. The Deakin Edge, a 450-seat indoor amphitheater, often stages free theater, comedy, talks and presentations, and cabaret.

*Clockwise from far left: The futuristic Federation Square is dominated by high-rise office buildings; the square is a popular gathering place for students; there's no shortage of watering holes in the square; the fragmented designs of the cultural buildings are reflected on the inside*

**Cultural square** While the prime attraction is the excellent Ian Potter Centre: NGV Australia (▷ 44), with its superb collections, the state-of-the-art, high-tech galleries, cinemas and studio spaces of the Australian Centre for the Moving Image (ACMI) will give you the lowdown on everything from more than a century of film history to the history of computer games and the latest digital art.

**Green spaces** The adjacent Birrarung Marr park lies on the north bank of the Yarra River and provides a link between the CBD and Melbourne's main sporting precinct. This contemporary park is part of a continuous green belt of parkland around the city. Festivals and events are held here along the river. The park also has a big children's playground.

## THE BASICS

fedsquare.com

✚ F7

✉ Corner of Flinders and Swanston streets

☎ 9655 1900

🕐 All hours, various times for museums. Visitor center daily 9–6

🍴 Cafés, restaurants and bars

🚇 Flinders Street

🚌 City Circle Tram

♿ Good

💰 Public areas free; admission to attractions

# Ian Potter Centre: NGV Australia

TOP 25

*The interior space of this superb gallery is almost as good as the collection itself*

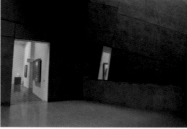

## THE BASICS

ngv.vic.gov.au
+ F6
✉ Federation Square
☎ 8620 2222
🕐 Daily 10–5
🍴 Crossbar Café
🚉 Flinders Street
🚊 City Circle Tram; 48, 70, 75
♿ Good
🎫 Free; charge for special exhibitions

## HIGHLIGHTS

● Aboriginal art
● Temporary exhibitions
● Tom Roberts' iconic *Shearing of the Rams*
● Emily Kngwarreye's classic work *Big Yam Dreaming*

**This stunning gallery, containing the world's largest collection of Australian art, plus special exhibitions, also has superb indigenous and nonindigenous art from the colonial period to the present day.**

**Indigenous art**  The Ian Potter Centre houses a collection of great depth and complexity. On display in 20 galleries over three levels, the collection of Australian art from the colonial period through to contemporary art, includes Aboriginal and Torres Strait Islander art, photography, prints and drawings, fashion and textiles, and decorative arts. There are over 800 works (from its collection of 20,000) displayed at any one time. The 19th-century section contains works by the Heidelberg School artists such as Arthur Streeton, and includes Tom Roberts' *Shearing of the Rams*. From the 20th century are works by Margaret Preston, Arthur Boyd, John Brack and Fred Williams. The Indigenous Art section contains works by William Barak, Ginger Riley and Lin Onus. It also includes Emily Kngwarreye's classic work *Big Yam Dreaming*.

**Room with a view**  The building is worth a visit in its own right. The interior spaces have been cleverly designed with shifting gallery view lines and cross connections giving a massive open feel; in contrast to this are enclosed calmer and darker galleries. Other sections are designed to open onto the landscape, with views across the Yarra River to the south.

# Immigration Museum

On board ship at the Immigration Museum (left); displays at the museum (right)

**Voices, images, letters and artifacts bring Victoria's immigration history to life in this contemporary museum. The former Customs Service building houses both the Hellenic Antiquities and Immigration museums.**

Hardships revisited  In this innovative museum special exhibitions sensitively explore themes of departure and arrival, journeys and settlement, and document the effects of immigration on Victoria since the early 1800s. Here you can walk through the re-creation of several ships' cabins and experience the cramped quarters endured by immigrants from the 1850s onwards on their way to Victoria. The Immigration Discovery Centre has a library that focuses on cultural heritage and immigration, where you can look up information on family history. Outside, at the rear of the museum, is the Tribute Garden, a memorial courtyard bearing the names of immigrants. It's worth a visit to the building alone, built between 1858 and 1870. The centerpiece of the museum is the elegant Long Room, a marvelous piece of Renaissance revival architecture, featuring 16 columns and a mosaic tile floor.

Galleries  The galleries on the first floor house temporary exhibitions run by local immigrant communities with the museum's support. Touring exhibitions from around the world are on the second floor, as well as a permanent exhibition about identity in Australia.

## THE BASICS

immigration.museum.vic.gov.au

✚ D7
✉ 400 Flinders Street
☎ 9927 2700
🕐 Daily 10–5
🍴 Café
🚇 Southern Cross or Flinders Street
🚋 City Circle Tram
♿ Good
👋 Inexpensive

## HIGHLIGHTS

● "Ship" experience
● The Long Room
● The Tribute Garden
● Immigration Discovery Centre
● Community cultural festivals

# Melbourne Aquarium

## HIGHLIGHTS

● Hand-feeding the sharks
● Mangrove and billabong exhibits
● Simulator rides
● Deep sea trench
● Themed retail outlet
● Dive school
● Walk-through tunnels
● Pinjarra, the saltwater crocodile

## TIP

● The aquarium can be crowded on school holidays and weekends.

**This popular CBD attraction includes a walk-through view of life under the southern oceans and a chance to watch divers hand-feeding sharks and rays. If you're feeling adventurous, join them in the Dive with Sharks program.**

**The aquarium** Start your visit on the ground floor, where a multitude of tanks feature the smaller marine creatures of the world's oceans. In this area, a huge floor-to-ceiling tank contains many Great Barrier Reef invertebrates and fish. After a break at the Adventurer's Cafe, you can proceed to the first floor for a close look at the rays and fish in the re-created mangrove ecosystem, and the long-necked turtles and eels in the billabong. The rock pool exhibit, also on this level, has hermit crabs, sea urchins,

*Clockwise from left: A giant ray at the Melbourne Aquarium; the waterside setting is home to one of the most popular attractions in the city; in the basement of the aquarium is the fascinating oceanarium, giving you a fish-eye view of an amazing underwater world*

starfish, sea cucumbers and other creatures that can be handled.

**The Mermaid Garden** For an insight into the diverse inhabitants of the Great Southern Ocean, walk down to the oceanarium, beneath the ground floor. Here you can walk along see-through tunnels, surrounded by a diverse array of sharks and rays, and talk to divers as they feed the fascinating inhabitants.

**Action stations** For an even more exhilarating experience, walk through the Croc Cave and see Pinjarra, a monster saltwater crocodile. Or try the Dive with Sharks program, if you dare. Slightly more sedate, but also exhilarating, are the King and Gentoo penguins splashing about in the Penguin Playground.

## THE BASICS

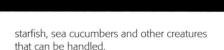

melbourneaquarium.
com.au
🚩 D7
✉ Corner of Flinders and King streets
☎ 9620 0999
🕐 Daily 9.30–6
🍴 Snack bar and licensed brasserie
🚉 Southern Cross or Flinders Street
🚋 City Circle Tram
♿ Very good
👋 Expensive
❓ Glass-bottom boat tours, special sessions for children/tour groups

47

# The Yarra River

*Central to the city is the beautiful Yarra River—take a boat trip for great views*

## THE BASICS

🞦 E7

✉ Melbourne River Cruises, Southgate

☎ 8610 2600; melbcruises.com.au

🕓 Daily

🚌 Various

💵 Walkways: free. Boat tours: moderate

## HIGHLIGHTS

● The walkways
● View from the Princes Bridge
● Picnic spots
● River cruises
● Cycleways
● Studley Park Boathouse
● Cruising restaurant
● City lights at night

**To the locals, the Yarra is the heart and soul of the city. Because of its murky color, it is known as the river that flows upside down. The winding waterway is perfect for a relaxing cruise.**

**The river** The Yarra is not particularly busy along the city center but you will often see tour boats cruising past. However, there's plenty going on where the river empties into Port Phillip Bay and a good place to absorb the scene is from the Princes Bridge, built in 1888. The best thing to do is to take a tour boat.

**The cruises** The down-river cruise meanders past the city CBD and Southbank, along the historical Victoria Docks, and on to the Docklands area. You can see Melbourne's lovely parks and gardens, as well as the stylish suburban architecture along the riverbanks. The Royal Botanic Gardens (▷ 60–61), Herring Island, Melbourne Olympic Park and the Melbourne Cricket Ground (▷ 74) are highlights of this trip. There are also combination tours, and alfresco dining aboard *The Spirit of Melbourne*.

**Riverside** Join Melbourne Bike Share at one of 50-odd city locations and cycle up or down the river on the excellent bicycle paths. Picnics along the grassy banks are a Melbourne tradition. To see the Yarra in a natural setting, don't miss Studley Park Boathouse at Kew, 6.5km (4 miles) from the city, where you can rent rowing boats and canoes.

# More to See

### DEGRAVES STREET

A bluestone cobbled laneway running between Flinders Street and Flinders Lane, Degraves is packed with café, bar and restaurant alfresco dining. A pink-tiled subway connects Degraves to Flinders Street Station. Boutique shops and art in glass cases line the subway walls.

🕂 E6 ⊠ Degraves Street 🚋 City Circle Tram

### FLINDERS STREET STATION

A wonder of French Renaissance architecture, Flinders Street Station was completed in 1909 and has since become a Melbourne icon. The steps under the dome's clocks are a famous meeting place for locals. The eye-catching yellow station is the busiest in Melbourne. The area around the station is a highlight of the White Night Festival as buildings are lit up with incredible projections.

🕂 F7 ⊠ Flinders Street ☎ 9610 7476 🕙 Daily 🚇 Flinders Street 🚋 City Circle Tram 🗓 Moderate

### ST. PAUL'S CATHEDRAL

stpaulscathedral.org.au

With its lofty spires and towers, beautiful stonework and magnificent stained glass, this Anglican cathedral is a classic example of Gothic revival architecture from the late 19th century. Inside you will see carved cedar woodwork, tiled floors and detailed stonework.

🕂 F6 ⊠ Corner of Swanston and Flinders streets ☎ 9650 4333 🕙 Daily 🚋 City Circle Tram 🗓 Free; tours expensive

### VICTORIA POLICE MUSEUM

policemuseum.vic.gov.au

This museum preserves old police records, photographs and artifacts from the 1800s. The museum reflects the diversity of work carried out by Victoria Police since the department was established in 1854 and displays period crime paraphernalia.

🕂 C7 ⊠ Mezzanine level, 637 Flinders Street ☎ 9247 5214 🕙 Mon–Fri 10–4 🚇 Flinders Street 🚋 City Circle Tram 🗓 Donation

*Degraves Street*

*St. Paul's Cathedral on the edge of Federation Square*

# Shopping

### CITY BASEMENT BOOKS
citybasementbooks.com.au
Quality secondhand books of every genre, topic and description.
➕ E7 ✉ 342 Flinders Street ☎ 9620 0428 🚋 City Circle Tram

### CITY HATTERS
cityhatters.com.au
An Akubra hat from this shop provides good protection from the sun.
➕ E7 ✉ 211 Flinders Street ☎ 9614 3294 🚋 City Circle Tram

### KOKO BLACK
kokoblack.com
Try the delicious hand-made chocolate products; favorites include Ice Cream Martini. Pralines, coffees, teas and hot chocolate are available at this popular shop.
➕ E7 ✉ Shop 4, Royal Arcade ☎ 9639 8911 🚋 City Circle Tram

### RETROSTAR VINTAGE CLOTHING
retrostar.com.au
Retrostar has the largest vintage clothing array in Australia, with a 1940s to 1980s rock-star section.
➕ F6 ✉ 1/37 Swanston Street ☎ 9663 1223 🚋 City Circle Tram

# Entertainment and Nightlife

### BEER DELUXE
beerdeluxe.com.au
This Federation Square bar with a huge beer garden serves beers, burgers and pizzas.
➕ F6 ✉ Federation Square ☎ 9663 0166 🕐 Daily 11.30am–midnight 🚋 City Circle Tram

### CHERRY BAR
cherrybar.com.au
Cherry Bar is Melbourne's premier rock 'n' roll venue.
➕ F6 ✉ 103 Flinders Lane ☎ 9639 8122 🕐 Mon–Wed 6pm–3am, Thu–Sat 5pm–5am, Sun 2pm–3am 🚋 City Circle Tram

### THE FORUM
forummelbourne.com.au
The Forum hosts concerts and other events.
➕ F6 ✉ Corner of Flinders and Russell streets ☎ 9299 9800 🚋 City Circle Tram

### RIVERLAND BAR AND CAFÉ
riverlandbar.com
Riverland offers stunning river views, a great wine list, a variety of draft beers from around the world, plus an interesting menu.
➕ E6 ✉ Vaults 1–9, Federation Wharf ☎ 9662 1771 🕐 Mon–Fri 10am–late, Sat–Sun 8am–late 🚋 City Circle Tram

**THEATER OFFERINGS**

Australian theater nurtured international stars such as Mel Gibson, Cate Blanchett, Geoffrey Rush and Toni Collette. You'll get a chance to see the stars of the future as well as view all kinds of dramatic entertainment at The Arts Centre (▷ 56), but look for performances by smaller theater companies at The Malthouse and La Mama Theatre. Lavish hit musical productions are performed at grand old venues such as the Princess Theatre (▷ 30, 37).

### TRANSPORT HOTEL
transporthotel.com.au
One of Melbourne's favorite pubs. Live music and DJs every night.
➕ F6 ✉ Corner of Princes Bridge and Northbank ☎ 9654 8808 🕐 Daily 11am–late 🚋 Flinders Street

### YOUNG AND JACKSONS
youngandjacksons.com.au
Melbourne's most famous pub is the location of *Chloe*, a nude painting that shocked the city in the late 19th century.
➕ F6 ✉ 1 Swanston Street ☎ 9650 3884 🕐 Daily 🚋 City Circle Tram

# Restaurants

## PRICES

Prices are approximate, based on a 3-course meal for one person.

| | |
|---|---|
| $ | A$20–A$40 |
| $$ | A$41–A$70 |
| $$$ | A$71–A$110 |

## ARINTJI ($$)

arintji.com.au

This restaurant has spectacular city and river views and something for all tastes—drinks, light meals, tapas or à la carte menu. Great cocktails and wine by the glass.
➕ F6 🗺 Corner of Swanston and Flinders streets ☎ 9663 9900 🕐 Daily 10am–late 🚋 City Circle Tram

## BLUE TRAIN CAFÉ ($)

bluetrain.com.au

The popular Blue Train Café offers tasty pizzas cooked in wood-fired ovens, and other light fare. The waiters clearly enjoy their work.
➕ E7 🗺 Mid-level, Southgate, Southbank (short walk from city center) ☎ 9696 0111 🕐 Breakfast, lunch and dinner daily

## BOKCHOY TANG ($$)

bokchoytang.com.au

Dine on contemporary Northern Chinese cuisine made with organic produce, where freshness and respect for the delicate, natural flavors of each ingredient are paramount. Panoramic views of the city.

➕ F6 🗺 Level 3, The Crossbar, Federation Square ☎ 9650 8666 🕐 Daily 11.30am–late 🚋 City Circle Tram

## CAFÉ CHINOTTO ($)

cafechinotto.com

This small café serves pizza, pasta and salads, with rapid and friendly service. Set on two levels, one looking out onto the Square and the other opening onto the Deakin Edge. Perfect for

a coffee or lunch break between sightseeing and shopping.
➕ F6 🗺 Federation Square ☎ 9650 8666 🕐 Daily 10am–late 🚋 City Circle Tram

## CODA BAR & RESTAURANT ($$$)

codarestaurant.com.au

Look for the laneway entrance to this stylish basement bar-restaurant that plates chef Adam D'Sylva's contemporary, seasonal innovations. Bookings are recommended, but walk-ins can sit at the bar.
➕ F6 🗺 141 Flinders Lane ☎ 9650 3155 🕐 Daily 12–3, 6–10.30 🚋 City Circle Tram

## CUMULUS INC ($$$)

cumulusinc.com.au

Acclaimed contemporary chef Andrew McConnell serves breakfast, lunch and dinner at this large bar and restaurant. High windows light up the classic interior.
➕ G6 🗺 45 Flinders Lane ☎ 9650 1445 🕐 Mon–Fri 7am–11pm, Sat–Sun 8am–11pm 🚋 City Circle Tram

## KENZAN ($$)

kenzan.com.au

Exceptional sushi and sashimi—one of the largest selections in the city—and excellent service in elegant surroundings make this place popular with locals and tourists.
➕ G5 🗺 45 Collins Street ☎ 9654 8933 🕐 Lunch and dinner Mon–Sat 🚋 City Circle Tram

South of the Yarra

Across the Princes Bridge are the leafy Royal Botanic Gardens, some fashionable suburbs and the entertainment precinct of Southbank, which includes the Crown Entertainment Complex, Southgate and the Arts Centre.

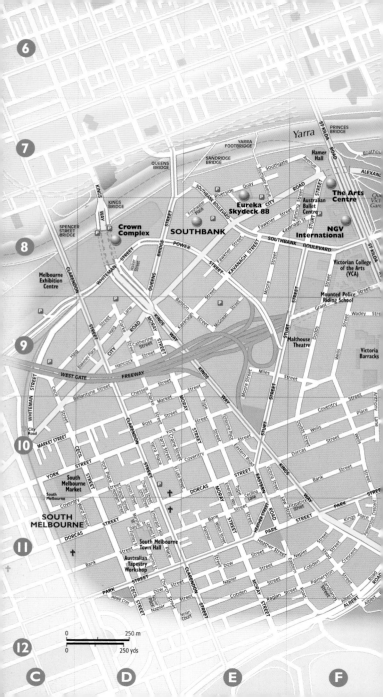

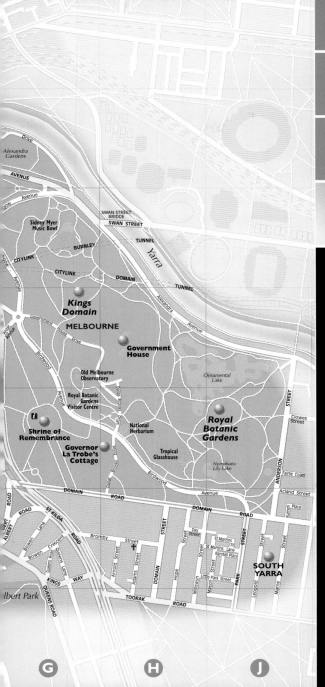

Alexandra Gardens

Drive

AVENUE

Avenue

SWAN STREET BRIDGE
SWAN STREET

Sidney Myer
Music Bowl

BURNLEY

TUNNEL

CITYLINK

Yarra

CITYLINK

DOMAIN

TUNNEL

Avenue

Alexandra

**Kings
Domain**

MELBOURNE

Government House Drive

Birdwood

**Government
House**

Old Melbourne
Observatory

Ornamental
Lake

Royal Botanic
Gardens Visitor Centre

Anderson Street

National
Herbarium

**Royal
Botanic
Gardens**

STREET

Clowes
Street

**Shrine of
Remembrance**

Dallas Brooks Drive

Tropical
Glasshouse

ANDERSON

Fairlie Court

**Governor
La Trobe's
Cottage**

Birdwood

Nymphaea
Lily Lake

Acland Street

DOMAIN

ROAD

Avenue

une Place

ROAD

DOMAIN

ROAD

PARK

ROAD

ALBERT

ST KILDA

Bromby

STREET

STREET

ay Street

ROAD

Bowen Lane

ROAD

Arnold Street

Hope Street

St Martins

Leopold Street

Bowen

Queens Lane

Crescent

Street

St Martins Lane

Street

Marne

Adams Street

Randall Place

Millswyn Street

Mason Street

**SOUTH
YARRA**

KINGS

QUEENS ROAD

WAY

DOMAIN

Little Park Street

Ibert Park

TOORAK

ROAD

**G**          **H**          **J**

# The Arts Centre

*Dominated by its elegant spire, the Arts Centre complex sits proudly by the river*

## THE BASICS

theartscentremelbourne.com.au

⊞ F7

✉ 100 St. Kilda Road

☎ Information: 9281 8000.
Ticketmaster: 1300 136 166

🕓 Daily 7–late

🍴 Cafés and bars

🚋 Tram 3, 5, 6, 8

♿ Good

👣 Moderate

❓ Guided tours daily, exhibitions, special tours and events. Check local press for current shows

## HIGHLIGHTS

● Elegant spire
● Location on the Yarra River
● Concert Hall
● Artworks
● Theatres Building
● Performing Arts Museum
● Guided tours

**The city's bastion of high culture is dominated by the webbed spire of the Theatres Building. The Hamer Hall, the State Theatre, the Playhouse and the Fairfax Studio are all found here.**

**Hamer Hall** This circular building next to the Yarra River is the city's main performing arts venue and home of the Melbourne Symphony Orchestra and the Australian Chamber Orchestra. The hall features a lavish interior, and a large collection of Australian art, and draws performers from around the world.

**Theatres Building** Linked to Hamer Hall by a walkway, this building houses the Playhouse, the State Theatre and the Fairfax Studio. The State Theatre features the world's largest mechanical stage. Overlooking the Yarra, next to Saké Restaurant & Bar, is The Channel, a community arts learning lab. Interesting and changing exhibitions of theater costumes, set designs and other memorabilia are held in the Centre foyers. Gallery 1, the major exhibition space, adjacent to the St. Kilda Road entrance, has exhibitions that complement The Arts Centre's performance program. The Playhouse Theatre foyers house a stunning collection of Western Desert paintings by important indigenous artists.

**Sidney Myer Music Bowl** This popular, outdoor summer venue, set in the nearby Kings Domain Gardens, hosts everything from rock concerts to opera soloists.

# Eureka Skydeck 88

*The huge Eureka Tower is topped by the Skydeck, for amazing views of the city*

**On the 88th level of the Eureka Tower, this observation deck includes a dramatic viewing experience in an extendable glass cube. It is Melbourne's tallest building at 300m (984ft).**

**What a view** While waiting for the high-speed elevators to take you up, examine the 6m (20ft), multiuser, interactive Serendipity Table that explores the stories and history of Melbourne. Once on the Skydeck, you are presented with a variety of viewing options. Besides the multidirectional glassed-in viewing sectors, there's a caged zone, The Terrace, where you can brave the outside elements.

**Close to The Edge** An additional thrill is available if you choose to purchase a ticket for The Edge—a 3m (10ft) square glass-cube that slides out from the building when it has its quota of brave souls on board. It's a weird sensation to be suspended 300m (984ft) above the ground. In poor weather conditions and high wind speeds, The Edge may not be operational. The Kiosk 88 serves drinks, snacks and ice creams; the gift shop has souvenirs and gifts.

**Statistics** Eureka Skydeck 88 was completed in 2006, taking four years to build at a cost of A$500 million. The 13 lifts, the fastest in the Southern Hemisphere, travel at more than 9m (30ft) per second. The top of the building can flex up to 600mm (2ft) in high winds.

## THE BASICS

eurekaskydeck.com.au

🔲 E7

✉ Riverside Quay, Southbank

☎ 9693 8888

🕐 Daily 10–10

🍴 Kiosk

🚇 Flinders Street

♿ Good

💲 Skydeck: expensive. The Edge: moderate

## HIGHLIGHTS

● Serendipity Table
● The Edge
● The Terrace
● Fine views

## TIP

● Forget The Edge if heights worry you.

# NGV International

## HIGHLIGHTS

- Asian art
- Dutch masters
- European art
- Sculpture courtyard
- Great Hall ceiling
- Decorative arts

## TIP

- The stained-glass ceiling of the Great Hall is best viewed by lying on your back.

**Australia's foremost art gallery has a vast selection of superb international art from Europe, Asia, America and Oceania. The collections of the NGV are regarded as the most comprehensive in Australia, and some works are world renowned.**

**International collection**  This much-loved local icon, designed by Sir Roy Grounds in the early 1960s, was once home to an extensive collection of Australian and international art, but the NGV International has now morphed into a gallery that features international art only. The gallery has more than 70,000 works of art, dating from 2,400BC to the present day, including pre-Columbian artifacts, Greek and Roman antiquities, and a fine collection of American paintings and sculpture. European Old Masters

*Exterior and interior views of the NGV International, which contains one of the greatest collections of international art in the world*

include Tiepolo, Rubens and Rembrandt, and there are also works by Rodin, Picasso, Monet and Henry Moore. Photography, prints, costumes, textiles and decorative arts from all periods are represented by exquisite examples, presented in elegant and dramatic surroundings. Particularly worth looking out for is the Leonard French stained-glass ceiling of the Great Hall, and the Asian art galleries.

**Temporary exhibitions** NGV International's diverse program of special exhibitions, in conjunction with national and international art museums, brings in the works of exceptional artists from around the world. The information desk has details of the lectures, floor talks, tours, films and children's activities on offer from time to time.

## THE BASICS

ngv.vic.gov.au

🚺 F8

✉ 180 St. Kilda Road

☎ 8620 2222

🕐 Wed–Mon 10–5

🍴 Restaurant and café

🚋 Tram 3, 5, 6, 8

♿ Excellent

✊ Free (charges for some exhibitions)

❓ Free tours daily, lectures, films, library and shop

# Royal Botanic Gardens

**One of the world's finest botanic gardens is a lovely place to be on a hot summer's day. Check out the free guided tours and open-air performances.**

**The gardens**  In 1857 the famous botanist Baron von Mueller was appointed director of these world-acclaimed gardens, which were established in 1846. Covering about 36ha (89 acres) they were superbly landscaped by William Guilfoyle, who curated them in the 18th-century English tradition with rolling lawns, formal flower gardens and wooded coppices. Today more than 12,000 plant species from around the world are in all stages of bud and blossom at any given time. From June to August the camellias are at their best. Between September and November roses, azaleas and

*Take a break from the busy city at the beautiful Royal Botanic Gardens*

rhododendrons bloom. On a summer's day, Fern Gully is a cool, tranquil spot beneath shady tree ferns. Don't miss the Australian rain-forest section, where many species are cultivated.

**Observatory Gate** This entrance to the gardens is the ideal orientation point for your visit. At the visitor center you can book a guided tour, browse the gardens, shop for unusual gifts and souvenirs, and enjoy breakfast, lunch or a snack in the excellent Jardin Tan kiosk and restaurant.

**Aboriginal Heritage Walks** On these walks, guides share their knowledge of the area and the life of the Bunurong and Woiwurrung people, who lived in the Melbourne area before Europeans arrived. You'll learn about their use of local plants, their culture and their history.

### THE BASICS

rbg.vic.gov.au

⊞ J10

✉ Birdwood Avenue

☎ 9252 2300. Aboriginal Heritage Walks: 9252 2429

🕓 Gardens: daily 7.30am–sunset. Aboriginal Heritage Walks: Thu–Sun 11am

🍴 Jardin Tan kiosk and restaurant

🚋 Tram 8

♿ Excellent

💲 Free

❓ Guided tours available

# Southbank and the Crown Complex

*This is the place for the latest in entertainment, dining and nightlife*

## THE BASICS

🚇 E8 (Southbank); D8 (Crown Complex)

✉ Crown Entertainment Complex, Southbank

☎ 9292 8888

🕐 Casino Complex: 24 hours daily

🍴 Cafés and restaurants

🚉 Flinders Street

🚋 Tram 10, 12, 96, 109

🚤 Boat tours on the Yarra

♿ Moderate

👆 Free

❓ Guided tours, night viewing and exhibitions

## HIGHLIGHTS

- River promenade
- Public art
- Shopping
- Cinemas
- Nightclubs
- Casino
- Restaurants
- Sunday market

**Melburnians come here in great numbers on weekends to stroll along the Yarra River, shop, dine at restaurants offering a wide choice of cuisines, and try their luck at the nearby Crown Casino.**

**Southbank** This riverside district across from the city center was once a dingy industrial area covered with warehouses and workshops. Now a popular spot for shopping and dining, many of Melbourne's attractions are located here, alongside the long-established Arts Centre and NGV International. Large sculptures line the riverbank and an arched footbridge joins Southbank's Southgate complex to the city. Look for the city's famous sculpture, *Ophelia*, by Melbourne artist Deborah Halpern. In summer, the arts festival sees free performances along Southbank.

**Crown Complex** Cinemas, cafés, cabarets and nightclubs make the Crown Entertainment Complex lively, especially on weekends. There are a lot of bars and restaurants with a range of cuisines and many specialist shops. Along the promenade, eight columns that overflow with water by day shoot fireballs at night.

**Crown Casino** Try your luck at pontoon, roulette, poker, pai gow and the Australian favorite, two-up. There are 300 gaming tables and 2,500 gaming machines in nine separate areas. Gambling is a serious issue in Victoria. Get help at responsiblegambling.vic.gov.au.

# More to See

### GOVERNMENT HOUSE

governor.vic.gov.au/government-house
Set within quiet gardens, this mansion was built in 1876 as the official residence of the Governor of Victoria. The interior is magnificently furnished and the ballroom is larger than the one at Buckingham Palace in London.

✚ H9 ✉ Government House Drive
☎ Tours: 9656 9804 🕐 Mon, Wed, Sat 10am, 1pm 🚊 Tram 8, 16 💷 Moderate

### GOVERNOR LA TROBE'S COTTAGE

This pretty little cottage, Victoria's first Government House, was brought from England in 1839 by Charles La Trobe, who became the first Lieutenant-Governor of the young colony. First set up at Jolimont, the building has been relocated and restored by Australia's National Trust, and many of the furnishings are original.

✚ H10 ✉ Birdwood Avenue ☎ 9656 9800 🕐 Daily 11–4 🚊 Tram 3, 5, 6, 8 ♿ Good 💷 Inexpensive

### KINGS DOMAIN

A major urban green space, the Kings Domain is also home to the Sidney Myer Music Bowl, the cottage of the first governor of Victoria, and the impressive Shrine of Remembrance. The Alexandra Gardens and Queen Victoria Gardens adjoin the outstanding 36ha (89-acre) Royal Botanic Gardens, and together form a continuous park between Princes Bridge and South Yarra. Features include monuments to Queen Victoria, King George V and a memorial to the remains of indigenous people.

✚ G9 ✉ St. Kilda Road ☎ 9654 5528 🕐 Daily 🚊 Tram 8, 16 ♿ Good 💷 Free

### SHRINE OF REMEMBRANCE

shrine.org.au
Melbourne's most recognized landmark is dedicated to those who died in World War I and to all the men and women who have served Australia.

✚ G10 ✉ Birdwood Avenue ☎ 9661 8100 🕐 Daily 10–5 🚊 Tram 3, 5, 6, 8 ♿ Good 💷 Free

### SOUTH YARRA AND PRAHRAN

One of the city's smartest areas, with its designer clothing, antiques, fine art, classy restaurants and people-watching. Explore Toorak Road and Chapel Street to get a sense of the place.

✚ J11/H12 and off map ✉ Toorak Road/Chapel Street 🍴 Many cafés, restaurants 🚊 Tram 1, 8

*Governor La Trobe's cottage*

# Domestic Architecture Walk

Melbourne's architectural heritage includes examples of elaborate ironwork, bluestone facades and decorative brickwork.

**DISTANCE:** 5km (3 miles)   **ALLOW:** 2 hours

**START** · · · · · · · ·

· · · · **END**

**FEDERATION SQUARE**
✚ F7  🚊 City Circle Tram

**SPRING STREET**
✚ G5  🚊 City Circle Tram

**❶** Begin at Federation Square (▷ 42–43), then hop on a City Circle Tram or walk to the corner of Spring Street and Treasury Gardens. Walk into the Gardens.

**❽** Walk to Spring Street and catch the City Circle Tram to your next destination.

**❷** Cross Lansdowne Street and pass the elegant 1930 conservatory on your way to Cook's Cottage. Continue towards Clarendon Street and cross into George Street.

**❼** At the end of Hotham is the impressive Bishopscourt, built in 1853 as the home for Anglican archbishops. Back in the Fitzroy Gardens you might like to stop at The Pavilion café (▷ 78) for a refreshment break.

**❸** Look for Hepburn Terrace at 199–209 George Street, a fine example of Victorian-era housing for the wealthy. Nearby, look for nos. 193 and 188.

**❻** Back on Powlett Street, nos. 158–164, called Cyprus Terrace, were designed to appear as four houses, but are really two homes.

**❹** These two well-restored 19th-century mansions are set opposite each other. Nearby, No. 182 dates from 1856. Cross Powlett Street to 109 George Street.

**❺** Here you will see a small 1930s-era block of flats. Walk to Simpson Street, turn left, then left again into Hotham, with Queen Bess Row, built in 1886, and the adjacent Sydenham House, once a girls' school.

SOUTH OF THE YARRA WALK

# Shopping

### ADRIANO ZUMBO
adrianozumbo.com
This patisserie is famous for its macaroons, plus cakes, tarts and all manner of pastries.
➕ Off map ✉ 14 Claremont Street, South Yarra ☎ 1800 858 6111 🚃 Tram 78, 79

### AQUA J
aquadecor.com.au
Art deco-inspired jewelry, including unique one-off creations.
➕ E7 ✉ Shop M7, Southgate (short walk from city center) ☎ 9696 6614

### DAKOTA 501
dakota501.com
This boutique denim retailer specializes in quality local and international denim labels including Levis, Lee, Diesel, Adidas and Autonomy.
➕ Off map ✉ 245 Chapel Street, South Yarra ☎ 9529 5546 🚃 Tram 8, 78

### DINOSAUR DESIGNS
dinosaurdesigns.com.au
Painted resin jewelry and homewares from Australia's top designers, Louise Olsen and Stephan Ormandy.
➕ Off map ✉ 562 Chapel Street, South Yarra ☎ 9827 2600 🚃 Tram 78, 79

### DOWNIES COINS
downies.com
Come here for coins and collectibles, stamps, jewelry and other gifts.
➕ E7 ✉ Shop U04, Southgate (short walk from city center) ☎ 9686 8411

### GREVILLE RECORDS
grevillerecords.com.au
Greville stocks a wide range of vinyl, plus books and rare paraphernalia.
➕ Off map ✉ 152 Greville Street, Prahran ☎ 9510 3012 🚃 Tram 78, 79

### GREVILLE VILLAGE MARKET
grevillevillagemarket.com.au
This market sells retro goods and all things alternative.
➕ Off map ✉ Greville Street, Prahran 🕐 1st and 3rd Sun of month 10–5 🚃 Tram 8, 78

### HAIGH'S CHOCOLATES
haighschocolates.com.au
The oldest family-owned chocolatier in Melbourne whips up bars, boxes and hampers of chocolates at this boutique store.
➕ Off map ✉ 499 Toorak Road, South Yarra ☎ 9827 8713 🚃 Tram 8

### UPMARKET SHOPS
Shops at the upper end of Collins Street, and in South Yarra and Toorak, sell international designer labels. Other international shops include Burberry, Bvlgari and Prada at the Crown Entertainment Complex, (▷ 62) and the Galleria Plaza shops. For fine jewelry fashioned from Australian pearls, opals, gold or diamonds, visit one of the jewelry shops.

### IAN SHARP
iansharp.com.au
Individually designed pieces of jewelry, including rings, bracelets, necklaces and earrings.
➕ Off map ✉ 65 Toorak Road, South Yarra ☎ 9866 4983 🚃 Tram 8

### JAM FACTORY
thejamfactory.com.au
Home to food outlets, a cinema complex and many specialist shops, this former jam factory is a destination in its own right.
➕ Off map ✉ 500 Chapel Street, South Yarra ☎ 9860 8500 🕐 Daily 10am–late 🚃 Tram 8

### KIRRA GALLERIES
kirragalleries.com
Fine Australian gifts, sculpture and decorative arts designed and hand-crafted in Australia.
➕ E7 ✉ Federation Square (short walk from city center) ☎ 9639 6388

### LE LOUVRE
lelouvre.com.au
Ever-changing fashion, art and design featuring international designer clothes by Valentino, Stella McCartney, Balmain and more.
➕ Off map ✉ 2 Daly Street, South Yarra ☎ 9650 1300 🚃 Tram 8, 78, 79

### MARY MARTIN BOOKSHOP
marymartinbooks.com.au
This shop has an excellent Australiana section.

➕ E7  ✉ Shop G17, Southgate, Southbank (short walk from city center) ☎ 9699 2292 🕐 Mon–Wed 10–6, Thu 10–7, Fri–Sat 10–10

## PALM BEADS
palmbeads.com.au
Semiprecious stones, silver and tribal jewelry from Asia and Africa.
➕ Off map  ✉ 181 Greville Street, Prahran ☎ 9510 1480 🚊 Tram 78, 79

## PRAHRAN MARKET
prahranmarket.com.au
This market near Chapel Street sells fresh produce and delicatessen goods.
➕ Off map  ✉ 163–185 Commercial Road ☎ 8290 8220 🕐 Tue, Thu, Sat 7–5, Fri 7–6, Sun 10–3 🚊 Tram 8, 72

## SAKS
saks.net.au
The latest trends from European designers include Alysi, Yasmin Velloza and Non e Vero.
➕ Off map  ✉ Shop 36B Malvern Central Shopping Centre ☎ 9500 8817 🚊 Tram 5

## SIGNED AND NUMBERED
signedandnumbered.com.au
Limited edition prints by Australian artists.
➕ Off map  ✉ 153 Greville Street, Prahran ☎ 9077 6468 🚊 Tram 78, 79

## SOUTHGATE
southgatemelbourne.com.au
This collection of shops and restaurants with great river views lies just across the Yarra River from the city center.
➕ E7  ✉ Southbank (short walk from city center)

## SOUTH MELBOURNE MARKET
southmelbournemarket. com.au
Everything from fresh fruit and vegetables to delicatessen items and household goods.
➕ C10  ✉ Corner of Cecil and York streets ☎ 9209 6295 🕐 Wed 8–4, Fri 8–5, Sat–Sun 8–4 🚉 South Melbourne 🚊 Tram 1, 12, 96, 109

## SOUTH YARRA & PRAHRAN
The stylish clothing shops and trendy restaurants of Chapel Street and Toorak Road are a big draw. Retro design and a gay subculture reign on Greville Street and Commercial Road.

### GEMS
Opals are the most popular gemstones sought out by visitors although you'll also find South Sea pearls, Argyle diamonds and original designs in Australian gold. Visit several shops to get an idea of the variety and price range before buying. Many shops have examples of rough stones and a few even have displays explaining the mining process. All are happy to answer questions.

➕ Off map  ✉ Chapel Street and Toorak Road, South Yarra; Greville Street and Commercial Road, Prahran 🚊 Tram 8, 78

## SOUTH YARRA ART HOUSE
syarthouse.com.au
Contemporary Australian art gallery and framer with many pieces for sale.
➕ Off map  ✉ 6 Almeida Crescent, South Yarra ☎ 9827 3771 🚊 Tram 78, 79

## THE SUNDAY ART MARKET
artscentremelbourne.com.au/ your-visit/sunday-market
Interesting and unusual handcrafted works.
➕ F7  ✉ The Arts Centre 🕐 Sun 10–4 🚉 Flinders Street

## SYBER'S BOOKS
sybersbooks.com.au
Full of rare and out-of-print books, including Australian literature.
➕ Off map  ✉ 38 Chapel Street, London ☎ 9530 2222 🚉 Windsor 🚊 Tram 78, 79

## THIRD WING
thirdwing.com.au
Jewelry, homewares and rare artifacts from around the world.
➕ Off map  ✉ Shop 2/180 Toorak Road, South Yarra ☎ 9826 6809 🚊 Tram 8

## VINTAGE SOLE
vintagesole.info
Handbags, vintage boots, belts and sheepskins.
➕ Off map  ✉ 153 Chapel Street, Windsor ☎ 9521 1175 🚊 Tram 8, 78

# Entertainment and Nightlife

## BELGIAN BEER CAFE

belgianbeercafemelbourne.com.au

This café serves Belgian and international beers.
➕ E7 ✉ Riverside Quay, Southbank (short walk from city center) ☎ 9690 5777 🕐 Daily 11am–1am

## BRIDIE O'REILLY'S

bridieoreillys.com.au

This popular Irish hotel serves all the favorites from the old country, plus good music, typical Irish decor and furnishings.
➕ Off map ✉ 462 Chapel Street, South Yarra ☎ 9827 7788 🕐 Mon–Wed 11–1am, Thu–Sat 11–3am 🚋 Tram 8, 78

## CHASERS

chasersnightclub.com.au

The latest dance music, old favorites and requests.
➕ Off map ✉ 386 Chapel Street, South Yarra ☎ 9827 7379 🕐 Nightly 🚋 Tram 8, 78

## CLUB 23

club23.com.au

Luxury club with crafted cocktails, rare whiskies and world-class DJs.
➕ D8 ✉ Level 3, Crown Towers, Crown Entertainment Complex, Southbank (short walk from city center) ☎ 9686 2323 🕐 Fri–Sat 6pm–late

## GROVE LIVE BAR & TERRACE

crownmelbourne.com.au/Groove-Live-Bar

Live music and comedy in luxury surroundings with '80s and '90s nights.

➕ D8 ✉ Level 1 Casino, Crown Entertainment Complex, Southbank (short walk from city center) ☎ 9292 8888 🕐 Thu 7pm–midnight, Fri–Sat 7pm–2.30am, Sun 7–10pm

## HAMER HALL

artscentremelbourne.com.au

Look for performances by the Melbourne Opera Company, Melbourne Symphony Orchestra and Australian Ballet.
➕ F7 ✉ The Arts Centre, Southbank ☎ 9281 8000 🕐 Call for tours 🚉 Flinders Street 🚋 Tram 3, 5, 6, 8

## MELBOURNE RECITAL CENTRE

melbournerecital.com.au

An architectural wonder with sensational acoustics. Showcases world-class music performances.
➕ F8 ✉ 31 Sturt Street,

### CLASSICAL CITY

The Arts Centre offers excellent opera, ballet and classical music. The world-renowned Melbourne Symphony Orchestra, Australian Ballet and Australian opera companies perform here regularly. The Melbourne Theatre Company has a regular season of productions at the State Theatre, while the complex's Playhouse presents a variety of theatrical productions. Classical music concerts are also given at the Town Hall and the Conservatorium of Music.

Southbank (short walk from city center) ☎ 9699 3333 🕐 Mon–Fri 9–5, plus evening events

## MELBOURNE SPORTS AND AQUATIC CENTRE

melbournesportshub.com.au/msac

A variety of swimming pools as well as a popular wave pool. Other sports include table tennis, basketball and volleyball.
➕ Off map ✉ Albert Park Road, Albert Park ☎ 9926 1555 🕐 Mon–Fri 6am–10pm, Sat–Sun 7am–8pm 🚋 Tram 12, 96

## P J O'BRIENS

pjobriens.com.au

A boisterous alternative to the standard high-tech venue. Faux Irish decor and live Irish music.
➕ E7 ✉ Southgate Complex (short walk from city center) ☎ 9686 5011 🕐 Nightly

## PONYFISH ISLAND

ponyfish.com.au

Floating bar kiosk beneath the Yarra River footbridge.
➕ E7 ✉ Southbank Pedestrian Bridge 🕐 Mon–Sat 8am–1am, Sun 10am–1am 🚋 City Circle Tram

## STATE THEATRE

artscentremelbourne.com.au

Opera Australia and the Australian Ballet perform on one of the largest stages in the world here.
➕ F7 ✉ The Arts Centre, Southbank ☎ 9281 8000 🕐 Shows: daily 🚉 Flinders Street 🚋 Tram 3, 5, 6, 8

# Restaurants

## PRICES

Prices are approximate, based on a 3-course meal for one person.

| | |
|---|---|
| $ | A$20–A$40 |
| $$ | A$41–A$70 |
| $$$ | A$71–A$110 |

## CAFFÈ E CUCINA ($$$)

caffeecucina.com.au
Long popular with the glitterati and deservedly so, since the Italian food here is always delicious.
🔼 Off map ✉ 581 Chapel Street, South Yarra ☎ 9827 4139 🕐 Lunch and dinner daily 🚋 Tram 8

## THE DECK ($)

thedeckrestaurant.com.au
This European-style brasserie overlooking the Yarra gives commanding views of the city skyline and serves light meals with great coffee.
🔼 E7 ✉ Southgate, Southbank (short walk from city center) ☎ 9699 9544 🕐 Breakfast, lunch and dinner daily 🚋 City Circle Tram

## FRANCE SOIR ($$$)

france-soir.com.au
A Melbourne landmark for more than 20 years, France Soir is consistently popular for its exquisite renderings of classic French dishes and extensive and varied wine list.
🔼 Off map ✉ 11 Toorak Road, South Yarra ☎ 9866 8569 🕐 Lunch and dinner daily 🚋 Tram 8

## THE GROOVE TRAIN ($)

groovetrain.com.au
Mediterranean, Modern Australian and international cuisines, plus pizza, vegetarian dishes, soups and seafood are served in a comfortable corporate atmosphere.
🔼 D11 ✉ 500 Chapel Street, South Yarra ☎ 9826 4444 🕐 Mon–Thu 7.30am–10.30pm, Fri–Sat 7.30am–11.30pm 🚋 Tram 8, 78

## ORITA'S ($$)

oritas.com.au
Upscale Japanese fusion cuisine with a must-try degustation menu.
🔼 Off map ✉ 34 Jackson Street, Toorak, South Yarra ☎ 9826 2111 🕐 Lunch Tue–Sat, dinner Tue–Sun 🚋 Tram 8

## THE POINT ($$$)

thepointalbertpark.com.au
A great location in Albert Park and stylish surroundings draw the crowds, as does the seasonal modern fare.
🔼 Off map ✉ Aquatic Drive, Albert Park ☎ 9682 5566 🕐 Lunch and dinner daily 🚋 Tram 12

## PURE SOUTH ($$)

puresouth.com.au
Modern Australian cuisine made with fresh, sustainable Tasmanian produce.
🔼 E7 ✉ Southgate Centre (short walk from city center) ☎ 9699 4600 🕐 Lunch Sun–Fri, dinner daily

## SAKÉ RESTAURANT ($$)

sakerestaurant.com.au
À la carte and banquet contemporary Japanese cuisine in the Hamer Hall part of the Arts Centre.
🔼 F7 ✉ Arts Centre, 100 St. Kilda Road ☎ 8687 0775 🕐 Daily noon–late 🚋 Tram 3, 5, 6, 8

## SEHERI ($$)

seherirestaurant.com.au
Modern Thai and Indian cooking keeps company with old favorites here.
🔼 Off map ✉ 209 Commercial Road, South Yarra ☎ 9827 3390 🕐 Dinner Tue–Sun 🚋 Tram 72

## SPITIKO RESTAURANT ($$)

spitiko.com.au
Traditional Greek meze, lamb on the spit and mixed grill.
🔼 Off map ✉ 270 Park Street, South Melbourne ☎ 9690 2600 🕐 Dinner Tue–Sun 🚋 Tram 1

## DINNER ON THE YARRA

What better way to experience Melbourne at night than a dinner cruise on the Yarra River? You definitely don't go for the food—it's the scenery, featuring the city skyline and docklands, that's the major draw. Operators include Melbourne River Cruises (☎ 8610 2600) for a dinner cruise and City River Cruises (☎ 9650 2214) will just provide the view.

Fringed by the lovely Fitzroy and Treasury Gardens, attractions eastwards of the CBD include the famous Melbourne Cricket Ground. Here, too, is Richmond, one of Melbourne's oldest suburbs.

**4**

**5**

**6**

**7**

**8**

NICHOLSON STREET

Evelyn
Place

P

**Fire
Services
Museum**

ALBERT

Yarra

0          250 m
0          250 yds

**E**          **F**          **G**

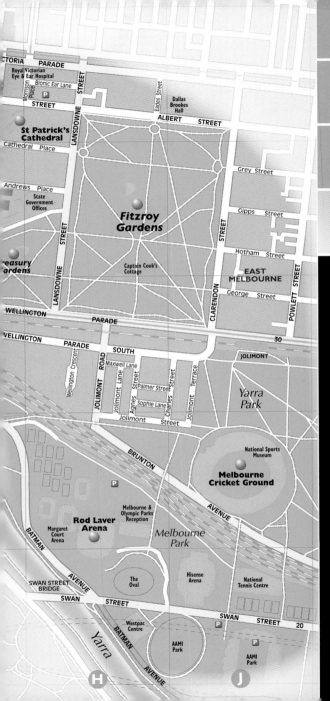

VICTORIA PARADE

Royal Victorian
Eye & Ear Hospital
Bionic Ear Lane

Morrison Place

STREET

LANSDOWNE STREET

Eades Street

Dallas
Brookes
Hall

ALBERT STREET

St Patrick's
Cathedral

Cathedral Place

Andrews Place

State
Government
Offices

Grey Street

Gipps Street

Treasury
Gardens

LANSDOWNE STREET

Fitzroy
Gardens

Captain Cook's
Cottage

Hotham Street

EAST
MELBOURNE

CLARENDON STREET

George Street

POWLETT STREET

WELLINGTON PARADE

WELLINGTON PARADE

SOUTH

30

JOLIMONT

Wellington Crescent

JOLIMONT ROAD

Maxwell Lane

Jolimont Lane

Agnes Street

Palmer Street

Sophie Lane

Charles Street

Jolimont Terrace

Jolimont Street

Yarra
Park

BRUNTON

National Sports
Museum

Melbourne
Cricket Ground

AVENUE

Rod Laver
Arena

Melbourne & 
Olympic Parks
Reception

Melbourne
Park

Margaret
Court Arena

BATMAN AVENUE

P

The
Oval

Hisense
Arena

National
Tennis Centre

SWAN STREET
BRIDGE

SWAN STREET

SWAN STREET

20

Westpac
Centre

Yarra

BATMAN AVENUE

AAMI
Park

P

AAMI
Park

H

J

# Fitzroy and Treasury Gardens

*Relax in the gardens and visit Captain Cook's pretty English-style cottage*

**The magnificent, tree-lined avenues of Fitzroy Gardens, designed in 1857, were laid out in the form of a Union Jack flag. A poignant memorial to former US President John F. Kennedy is the centerpiece of the nearby Treasury Gardens.**

**Fitzroy Gardens** Fitzroy Gardens, with partly hidden glades, waterfalls and shady avenues of elms forming canopies across the pathways, is the location of Cook's Cottage. Also within the gardens is the Fairy Tree, whose trunk is carved with fantasy figures and Australian animals, a conservatory and the miniature Tudor Village, which was presented to Melbourne by the people of Lambeth, London, in appreciation of food packages sent to Britain by Melburnians after World War II.

**Cook's Cottage** This small, typically English cottage, dating from 1755, was the home of the parents of navigator, Captain James Cook. Dismantled, it was shipped from Yorkshire to Melbourne in 1934 to be erected, stone by stone, on this site. Furnished in the style of the period, it contains an interpretive area that explores the life of James Cook.

**Treasury Gardens** At lunchtime, many city workers frequent this pleasant, tranquil park planted with poplars, elms, oaks and cedars. There is a memorial to US President John F. Kennedy at the edge of the gardens' pretty ornamental lake.

## THE BASICS

fitzroygardens.com
H5 and G5
Off Wellington Parade
Cook's Cottage: 9658 9658
Cook's Cottage: daily 9–5
Restaurant
Jolimont
Tram 48, 75
Moderate

## HIGHLIGHTS

- Avenues of trees
- Conservatory
- Fairy Tree
- Model Tudor village
- Cook's Cottage
- John F. Kennedy Memorial
- The Pavilion restaurant

# Melbourne Cricket Ground

*Modern design meets traditional cricket at the Melbourne Cricket Ground*

## THE BASICS

mcg.org.au

✚ J7

✉ Jolimont Street

☎ 9657 8888

🕙 Daily 10–3

🚆 Jolimont, Richmond

🚋 Tram 48, 70, 75

♿ Poor

🍴 Moderate

❓ Tours depart hourly from inside Gate 3, from 10–3 on non-event days

## HIGHLIGHTS

● Standing on the oval
● Members' Pavilion
● Interactive games
● Olympic Museum
● Australian Gallery of Sport

**Many Melburnians live for sport, especially cricket and their beloved Australian Rules Football. This 100,000-seat arena has long been the epicenter of these two sports in the city and was the focal point of the 1956 Olympics.**

**The hallowed ground** Each week of the season, football followers deck themselves out in their team colors and flock to the MCG. If you are in Melbourne, attend a football or cricket match and soak up the atmosphere—few stadiums in the world generate the excitement of the MCG. A guided tour is always a must: you can sit in the room where the team watches the game, visit the Long Room hung with portraits of cricketing greats, and inspect the memorabilia-packed Melbourne Cricket Club Museum. For many, a tour highlight is to stand on the famous playing field.

**Olympic Museum** This major International Olympic Committee-endorsed museum traces the history of the modern games. There are photographic displays of each of the modern Olympics, with priceless items of memorabilia such as wild olive branches won at Athens in 1896 and various gold medals.

**Australian Gallery of Sport** Perhaps the best way to learn about cricket and Australian Rules Football is to visit this gallery, in the same complex, which includes the Australian Cricket Hall of Fame and hosts temporary exhibitions.

# More to See

### FIRE SERVICES MUSEUM
fsmv.net.au
On the ground floor of a 19th-century fire station, this museum houses a collection of firefighting memorabilia such as uniforms and photographs, and includes Australia's largest collection of restored fire trucks. It's the biggest array of fire equipment in the Southern Hemisphere, spanning several hundred years.
⊕ G4 ✉ 39 Gisborne Street ☎ 9662 2907 ⏰ Thu–Fri 9–3, Sun 10–4 🚋 City Circle Tram, 11, 12, 109 from Collins Street ✋ Inexpensive

### RICHMOND
In Richmond, one of the city's oldest suburbs and a short tram ride from the CBD, you can find fashion outlets, with designer seconds, and some great Greek food. Vietnamese culture thrives on Victoria Street, Melbourne's Little Saigon.
⊕ Off map at J8 ✉ Bridge Road, Swan Street and Victoria Street 🍴 Many cafés and restaurants 🚋 Tram 48, 75, 109

### ROD LAVER ARENA
rodlaverarena.com.au
One of Australia's largest sporting and entertainment venues is named after legendary Australian tennis player Rod Laver. Seating around 15,000, the arena attracts around a million visitors to events each year, including the annual prestigious Australian Open tennis event.
⊕ H7 ✉ Batman Avenue, Melbourne and Olympic Park precinct ☎ 9286 1600 ⏰ Events vary, call for information 🚉 Flinders Street 🚋 Tram 48, 70, 75 ✋ Expensive

### ST. PATRICK'S CATHEDRAL
cam.org.au/cathedral
You can see the spires of this 1897 bluestone Catholic cathedral from points all over the city. The interior has soaring, slender pillars, stained-glass windows and mosaic floor tiles. Exquisite glass mosaics are set into the marble and alabaster altars.
⊕ G4 ✉ Cathedral Place ☎ 9662 2233 ⏰ Mon–Fri 7–4, Sat–Sun 8–5 🚋 City Circle Tram, 24, 48, 75, 109 ✋ Free

*Detail from the community project mural in Stephenson Street, Richmond*

# Shopping

### BONDS OUTLET
bondsoutlet.com.au
This factory outlet sells Bonds clothing, including socks, underwear and lingerie. The outlet also stocks top fashion brands such as Berlei, Jockey, Holeproof, Mossimo and Mooks.
➕ Off map  ✉ 221 Bridge Road and Swan Street, Richmond  ☎ 9427 8772
🚊 Tram 48, 75

### RICHMOND
Apart from the suburb's Greek and Vietnamese shops, Bridge Road and Swan Street offer designer seconds outlets and other shopping experiences. It makes a pleasant change to get out of the city to this vibrant suburb.
➕ Off map  ✉ Bridge Road and Swan Street, Richmond
🚊 Tram 48, 75, 109

### RICHMOND HILL CAFÉ AND LARDER
rhcl.com.au
Fine condiments and fresh produce are for sale here, as well as a huge selection of cheeses. They also have cheese night events. The place doubles as a café serving tasty, fresh meals.
➕ Off map  ✉ 48 Bridge Road, Richmond  ☎ 9421 2808  🚊 Tram 48, 75

# Entertainment and Nightlife

### BASKETBALL
melbourneutd.com.au
The Melbourne Park Complex is the home of NBL basketball team Melbourne United, who take part in national competitions.
➕ J8  ✉ Melbourne Park Complex  ☎ 9099 5500  ◉ Oct–Apr usually Fri, Sat
🚊 Tram 48, 70, 75

### CORNER HOTEL
cornerhotel.com
Listen to a great range of cutting-edge music at this Melbourne institution.
➕ Off map  ✉ 57 Swan Street, Richmond  ☎ 1300 724 867  ◉ Most nights
🚊 Tram 70

### ROYAL OAK HOTEL
royaloakrichmond.com.au
This traditional pub has a large-screen TV showing sporting events, and a small TAB (betting shop)

means you can place a bet. A bistro has nightly specials.
➕ Off map  ✉ 527 Bridge Road, Richmond  ☎ 9428

---

#### WATERING HOLES

When white settlers first established towns in Australia, the pub was often the first substantial building to be erected. Today there are countless pubs and bars. Melburnians love craft beers and Mountain Goat and Two Birds are top choices. Make the most of bar food and beer and order a "pot and a parma" (a glass of beer and a chicken parmigiana). The rooftops and laneways are loaded with cocktail bars. Most bars are open until 1am and nightclubs open into the early hours.

---

4200  ◉ Daily 10am–late
🚊 Tram 48, 75

### SPREAD EAGLE HOTEL
spreadeagle.com.au
This bustling corner pub has a comprehensive beer, wine and spirit list, and a bistro serving traditional pub fare.
➕ Off map  ✉ 372 Bridge Road, Richmond  ☎ 9428 6895  ◉ Daily 11am–11.45pm  🚊 Tram 48, 75

### THE SWAN HOTEL
theswan.com.au
A traditional pub and the perfect venue to enjoy live music. Serves great pub meals and has a spacious beer garden. Friday and Saturday nights feature an in-house DJ.
➕ Off map  ✉ 425 Church Street, Richmond  ☎ 9428 2112  ◉ Daily noon–late
🚊 Tram 48, 70, 78, 109

# Restaurants

## PRICES

Prices are approximate, based on a 3-course meal for one person.

| | |
|---|---|
| $ | A$20–A$40 |
| $$ | A$41–A$70 |
| $$$ | A$71–A$110 |

## BURMESE HOUSE ($$)

burmesehouse.com.au
Burmese music in the background, an open kitchen in the middle, and friendly staff create an unforgettable atmosphere. Be sure to try the egg noodles and chicken coconut curry.
➕ Off map ✉ 303 Bridge Road, Richmond ☎ 9421 2861 🕐 Lunch Mon–Sat 11.30–2.30, dinner daily 5.30–10 🚋 Tram 48, 75

## THE COMMUNE ($)

thecommune.com.au
Popular as a casual lunch spot, with a great range of savory pastries, baguettes and focaccias. Thursday night is jazz night.
➕ Off map ✉ 2 Parliament Place, East Melbourne ☎ 9654 5477 🕐 Mon–Fri 7.30–5.30 🚋 Tram 12, 109

## FENIX ($$$)

fenix.com.au
This outstanding riverside restaurant offers dishes composed of unusual ingredients, plus steaks, grilled fish and salads. Reservations required.
➕ Off map ✉ 680 Victoria Street, Richmond ☎ 9427 9257 🕐 Mon–Sat 9–5 🚋 Tram 12, 109

## GEORGE STREET CAFÉ ($)

georgestreetcafe.com.au
Hearty breakfasts and lunches and outside seating for warmer days. The Bircher muesli with fresh fruit salad is a breakfast special.
➕ Off map ✉ 65 George Street, East Melbourne ☎ 9419 5805 🕐 Mon–Fri 7–3, Sat–Sun 8–3 🚋 Tram 48, 75

## MINH TAN II ($)

A huge menu of Chinese and Vietnamese dishes, with especially good seafood, makes this no-frills restaurant popular.
➕ Off map ✉ 190 Victoria Street, Richmond ☎ 9427 7131 🕐 Daily 10.30–10.30 🚋 Tram 12, 109

## NOIR ($$$)

noirrestaurant.com.au
Modern French cuisine is served at this stylish

### VICTORIAN WINES

It's worth seeking out Victorian wines to go with your food, particularly those from the Yarra Valley and Macedon Ranges. Wines from the Yarra Valley include Chardonnay and Pinot Noir; Macedon Ranges include Merlot and Cabernet Sauvignon. Good winemakers to look for include De Bortoli, Yering Station, Best's, Diamond Valley, Mount Macedon and Mount Gisborne.

restaurant; arrive early and relax in the sophisticated wine bar above. Reservations advised.
➕ Off map ✉ 175 Swan Street, Richmond ☎ 9428 3585 🕐 Mon–Thu 6–10pm, Fri–Sun noon–10 🚋 Tram 48, 75

## THE PAVILION ($$)

thepavilionfitzroygardens. com.au
Set in an ornamental garden in the historic Fitzroy Gardens, there is plenty of tasty café-style fare on offer here.
➕ Off map ✉ Fitzroy Gardens, East Melbourne ☎ 9417 2544 🕐 Daily 9–5 🚋 Tram 48, 75

## RADII ($$$)

Extravagant decor and high-class culinary creations. Watch your meal being prepared in the open kitchen, from a menu of fresh, seasonal European dishes.
➕ Off map ✉ Park Hyatt Hotel 1, Parliament Square, East Melbourne ☎ 9224 1211 🕐 Breakfast daily, dinner Mon–Sat 🚋 Tram 11, 12, 109

## RICHMOND HILL CAFÉ & LARDER ($$)

rhcl.com.au
Enjoy the contemporary, Mediterranean-style dishes, efficient service and excellent cheese shop. Breakfast until 3pm.
➕ Off map ✉ 48–50 Bridge Road, Richmond ☎ 9421 2808 🕐 Daily 8–5 🚋 Tram 48, 75

These lively inner-city suburbs are easily reached by tram from the CBD. Carlton, with its excellent museum, has good eateries, bookshops and galleries, while eclectic Fitzroy exudes an alternative atmosphere.

| | |
|---|---|
| Sights | 82–86 |
| Walk | 87 |
| Shopping | 88 |
| Entertainment and Nightlife | 89 |
| Restaurants | 90 |

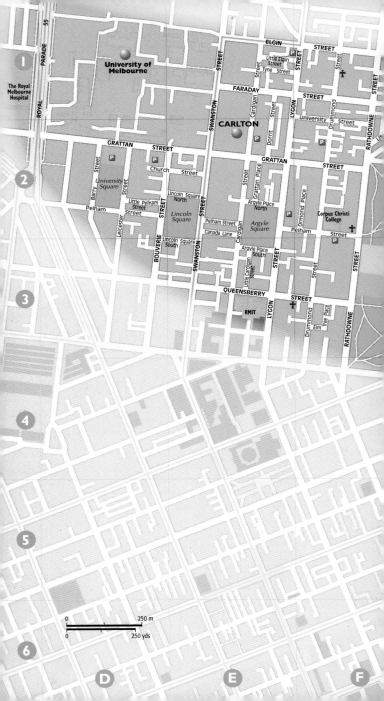

# Carlton

*Carlton is popular for eating out—Lygon Street (left) and University Café (right)*

## THE BASICS

➕ E2
✉ Lygon Street, Rathdowne Street
🍴 Many cafés and restaurants
🚋 Tram 1, 8

## HIGHLIGHTS

- Italian culture
- Restaurants
- Nightlife
- Specialty shopping

**This trendy suburb, a short walk north of the CBD and close to Melbourne University, has long been dubbed the city's Little Italy. Its epicenter is bustling Lygon Street, with its alfresco dining scene.**

**Tasty Italian** Carlton's Italian origins date from the early 1900s, when Italian migrants settled here, and were boosted with post-World War II migration. It is the perfect near-city destination for a gastronomic expedition, since there are any number of excellent eating places to tempt you. In old double-storied Victorian terraced houses, restaurants literally spill onto the footpath, their colorful umbrellas providing shelter and busy waiters serving bowls of pasta and espressos to appreciative diners.

**Lots to do** Besides delicious Italian fare, you'll find boutiques, specialty men's and women's clothing shops, jewelry shops and gift and design shops on a leisurely stroll. Try to catch a performance at La Mama Theatre (▷ 89), one of Melbourne's original experimental theaters, where productions are often new works showcasing up-and-coming writers and actors.

**More delights** There are also art cinemas, bookshops and galleries, and Lygon Street has one of the best bookshops in Melbourne, Readings (▷ 88). At the northern end of Argyle Street is Piazza Italia, with gardens, stone paving and a huge solar clock. Here you can sit in the sun, close your eyes, and dream of being in Italy.

Bohemian lifestyles
and festival parades
are central to the
suburb of Fitzroy

**A casual walk along Fitzroy's lively Brunswick Street, with its fascinating people, quirky stores, excellent restaurants and exciting nightlife, provides a glimpse of an alternative Melbourne.**

**Multicultural** Once a fashionable residential area, Fitzroy has since gone through phases of working-class and immigrant inhabitants. Today the area is increasingly occupied by some of Melbourne's vibrant subcultures, including students and artists, along with trendy, inner-city urbanites attracted by the suburb's eclectic nature. Part of the fun of hanging out here is to sit with a coffee and people-watch. For shopping, the area is hard to beat; it's a great place to buy books, art, antiques and the latest retro fashions. Melbourne's Spanish community is based in nearby Johnson Street, where you will find specialist eating places, grocery shops and gift shops. You'll also find food of every variety—Turkish, Greek, Italian, Thai, Malaysian, Vietnamese and Tibetan—especially around the junction with Johnson Street. There are plenty of restaurants featuring Modern Australian cuisine, too. For the best choice head for places with a crowd—the local stamp of approval.

**Melbourne's art scene** If you are interested in art, find your way to Gertrude Street, where Melbourne's emerging artists show their work. You'll also find some retro fashion and cutting-edge clothing shops here, along with more hip coffee shops.

## THE BASICS

➕ H2
✉ Brunswick Street
🍴 Cafés and restaurants
🚊 Tram 11
♿ Fair

## HIGHLIGHTS

- People-watching
- Bric-a-brac shops
- Designer clothes shops
- Nightlife
- Art galleries

**CARLTON AND FITZROY TOP 25**

# Melbourne Museum

Melbourne's Children's Museum (left); Aboriginal panels in the main museum (right)

## THE BASICS

museumvictoria.com.au/
melbournemuseum

☥ F3

✉ 11 Nicholson Street,
Carlton Gardens, Carlton

☎ 13 11 02/8341 7777

🕐 Daily 10–5

🍴 Café and restaurant

🚃 City Circle Tram, 86, 96

♿ Excellent

💲 Inexpensive

❓ Guided tours

**IMAX theater**

imaxmelbourne.com.au

✉ Rathdowne Street,
Carlton

☎ 9663 5454

## HIGHLIGHTS

● Bunjilaka Aboriginal
Centre
● Decorative Arts section
● Children's Discovery
Centre
● IMAX cinema
● Forest Gallery
● Science Gallery
● Te Pasifika Gallery

**This ultra-modern museum features the art, culture and natural history of Melbourne and the surrounding area, using interaction, performance and the latest technology.**

**Museum exhibitions** Major touring exhibitions supplement the collections of this museum in Carlton Gardens, opposite the grand 19th-century Royal Exhibition Building. The Bunjilaka Aboriginal Centre tells the stories of Victorian Aborigines, and explores the land and issues relating to Aboriginal laws, traditional knowledge and property. The Melbourne Gallery focuses primarily on the city's history. Te Pasifika Gallery houses art from many Pacific countries.

**Our world** In the Forest Gallery you walk among living trees, plants, animals, birds and insects; five interpretive zones explain the effects of fire, water, earth movement, climate and humans on the forests around Melbourne. Exhibitions in the Science and Life Gallery show how much science shapes our world. Technology exhibitions explore the rapid evolution of digital technology and its dramatic effects on our daily lives. Check out the intricate workings of human beings in the popular Mind and Body Gallery.

**Family fun** Nearby at the Children's Museum, in a colorful, cube-shaped building known as the Big Box, kids and their families are encouraged to engage with interactive exhibitions. The IMAX cinema, shops and cafés are in the complex.

# Melbourne Zoo

*Placid giraffes, bathing elephants and lowland gorillas are just some of the creatures at the zoo*

**Gorillas get top billing here, but the otters are just as fascinating, as are kangaroos, koalas and wombats. The platypus is also represented, together with much of Australia's unique birdlife.**

**Background** This popular zoo, the third oldest in the world and first in Australia, was established in 1862 in Royal Park. At first the zoo was used by The Acclimatisation Society as a recovery center for domestic livestock after their grueling 16-week sea passage. After 1870, more exotic animals were collected for display.

**Australian fauna** Today the zoo exhibits more than 320 animal species from Australia and around the world, most housed in landscaped enclosures. Platypuses caper in the nocturnal display and fur seals glide past in an underwater environment. Even the gorillas have their own rain forest. Come face-to-face with the kings of the jungle in Lion Gorge. Sumatran tigers, otters and pygmy hippopotamuses star in the innovative African and Asian zones.

**Royal Park** The zoo is the focal point of this park. There are hockey and netball stadiums here, as well as facilities for cricket, football, tennis and golf. Elsewhere, green open spaces, shady roads, gardens of native plants and groves of smooth eucalyptus trees make you feel far away from busy Melbourne. Look for the memorial cairn to Burke and Wills, commemorating the fateful crossing of the Australian interior in 1860.

## THE BASICS

zoo.org.au/melbourne
✚ Off map at D1
✉ Elliot Avenue, Parkville
☎ 9285 9300
🕐 Daily 9–5
🍴 Variety of cafés and kiosks
🚉 Royal Park
🚋 Tram 19, 55
♿ Good
👍 Moderate
❓ Guided tours, nocturnal tours, special zoo-keeper presentations and talks

## HIGHLIGHTS

● Western lowland gorillas
● Sumatran tigers
● Australian mammals
● Butterfly House
● Japanese Garden
● Platypus nocturnal display
● Royal Park
● Twilight concerts

# More to See

### CARLTON AND UNITED BREWERIES

carltonbrewhouse.com.au

Visit Carlton Brewhouse for a tour of an Australian brewery. It includes a look at the production, bottling and keg lines, before returning to the tasting room to sample different beers. There is a café for refreshments. Bookings are essential.

✚ Off map at H4　✉ Corner of Nelson and Thompson streets, Abbotsford　☎ 9420 6800　🕐 Tours Mon–Sat at 10, 2　🚋 Tram 109　✋ Moderate

### CARLTON GARDENS

museumvictoria.com.au/reb/history/carlton-gardens/

These gardens are well laid out with public art, a huge fountain and avenues of mature trees. In the center is the Royal Exhibition Building, built for the Melbourne International Exhibition of 1880 and still used for trade shows. Next to Carlton Gardens, in Nicholson Street, is a restored row of terraced houses, known as Royal Terrace. The innovative Melbourne Museum is next to the gardens to the north.

✚ F2/F3　✉ Between Rathdowne and Nicholson streets　🚋 City Circle Tram　✋ Free

### ROYAL EXHIBITION BUILDING

museumvictoria.com.au/reb

A UNESCO World Heritage building, this magnificent structure was built for the International Exhibition of 1880 and remains the world's oldest surviving structure of its type.

✚ F3　✉ Nicholson Street, Carlton　☎ 13 11 02　🕐 Tours daily at 2　🚋 Trams 86, 96　✋ Inexpensive

### UNIVERSITY OF MELBOURNE

unimelb.edu.au

Wander around these attractive grounds and admire the buildings, including Ormond College (1880), with its Gothic tower, and Newman College, designed in 1918 by the architect Walter Burley Griffin.

✚ D1　✉ Grattan Street, Parkville　☎ 9035 5511　🕐 Daily　🍴 Several cafés　🚋 Tram 1, 16　✋ Free

*Carlton Gardens is home to the modern Melbourne Museum*

*Royal Exhibition Building, Carlton Gardens*

# Carlton Gardens to Lygon Street

This interesting walk includes the grand old Royal Exhibition Building, the Melbourne Museum and bustling Lygon Street.

**DISTANCE:** 3km (2 miles)    **ALLOW:** 3 hours

**START**
**CARLTON GARDENS**
✚ F4  🚋 Tram 86, 96

**1** Begin at Carlton Gardens South on the corner of Victoria and Rathdowne streets, walk diagonally across towards the Royal Exhibition Building (▷ 86), to the Hochgurtel Fountain, with its three colossal half-man, half-fish figures.

**2** Walk to the east around the building past the French fountain with its three figures supporting dolphins, to take in the scale of this impressive building.

**3** Just opposite is the dramatic Melbourne Museum (▷ 84). You can't miss the huge indoor forest as you enter the building.

**4** Now walk westwards past the IMAX theater and the colorful cube building into the northern section of Carlton Gardens (▷ 86).

**END**
**LYGON STREET**
✚ E2  🚌 Buses 200, 207

**8** From here you can catch the bus back into the CBD.

**7** Make your way southwards, along Lygon Street, to the intersection of Pelham and Lygon streets, where you'll find the Piazza Italia and the adjacent pretty Argyle Square.

**6** At 380 Lygon Street, there is a good collection of specialty shops in the Lygon Court Shopping Piazza, which also houses one of Melbourne's finest art-house cinemas.

**5** Walk down Rathdowne Street, turn left into Grattan Street, then walk the two blocks to Lygon Street.

**CARLTON AND FITZROY WALK**

# Shopping

### ALPHA60
alpha60.com.au
Sophisticated, quirky clothing for men and women.
🚩 H1 ✉ 262 Brunswick Street, Fitzroy ☎ 9416 4296
🚃 Tram 11

### BRUNSWICK STREET BOOKSTORE
brunswickstreetbookstore.com
This eclectic shop has all the latest titles and more, plus plenty of places to sit and read.
🚩 H2 ✉ 305 Brunswick Street, Fitzroy ☎ 9416 1030
🚃 Tram 11

### CARLTON
Follow your nose to delicious coffee and fresh pasta on Lygon Street, Melbourne's own Little Italy. Check out the great shopping in the surrounding area.
🚩 E2 ✉ Lygon Street, Carlton 🚃 Tram 1, 8, 96

### DENIM DELUXE
denimdeluxe.com.au
This denim superstore offers a great range of street wear and skate wear, plus sale jeans and brand labels at reduced prices.
🚩 J1 ✉ 397 Smith Street, Fitzroy ☎ 9486 9050
🚃 Tram 86

### FITZROY
The way-out shops on Brunswick Street reflect the alternative nature of the suburb. Good for fashion, books and galleries.
🚩 H2 ✉ Brunswick Street, Fitzroy 🚃 Tram 11

### ISHKA HANDCRAFTS
ishka.com.au
Handcrafts from developing communities globally—gifts, homeware, jewelry and furniture.
🚩 G1 ✉ 300 Nicholson Street, Fitzroy ☎ 9416 0777
🚃 Tram 96

### MAKE DESIGNED OBJECTS
makedesignedobjects.com
Quality local and internationally designed objects from Ittala, Rosendahl, Fink & Co!, Menu and Evasolo.
🚩 E1 ✉ 194 Elgin Street, Carlton ☎ 9347 4225
🚃 Tram 1

### MUSIC SWOP SHOP
musicswopshop.com.au
Lots of secondhand and rare musical instruments are for sale here; also custom instrument design and repairs.
🚩 E1 ✉ 147 Elgin Street, Carlton ☎ 9348 1194
🚃 Tram 1

### THE ORIGINAL LOLLY STORE
theoriginallollystore.com.au
American, English and Dutch sweets, European chocolates, plus good old Australian favorites.
🚩 E2 ✉ 239 Lygon Street, Carlton ☎ 9347 5641
🚃 Tram 1, 8

### POLYESTER
polyesterrecords.com
This independent record store stocks a huge range of vinyl, CDs, DVDs and books.
🚩 Off map ✉ 387 Brunswick Street, Fitzroy
☎ 9419 5137 🚃 Tram 11

### QUICK BROWN FOX
quickbrownfox.com.au
Choose from a huge range of colorful women's clothing, glamorous handbags, shoes, wallets and jewelry at the top end of Brunswick Street.
🚩 Off map ✉ 375 Brunswick Street, Fitzroy
☎ 8415 1992 🚃 Tram 11

### READINGS
readings.com.au
One of Melbourne's top bookshops, Readings sells an excellent range of the latest titles and CDs.
🚩 E2 ✉ 309 Lygon Street, Carlton ☎ 9347 6633
🚃 Tram 1, 8

### ROSE STREET ARTISTS' MARKET
rosestmarket.com.au
Find high-quality, locally designed jewelry, clothes, accessories, art, vintage pieces, collectibles, homewares and soft furnishings here.
🚩 Off map ✉ 60 Rose Street, Fitzroy ☎ 9419 5529
🕐 Sat–Sun 11–5 🚃 Tram 11

### TOMORROW NEVER KNOWS
tomorrowneverknows.com.au
Melbourne designers offer casual clothing for men and women, plus the coolest T-shirts in Melbourne.
🚩 Off map ✉ 415 Brunswick Street, Fitzroy
☎ 9495 6645 🚃 Tram 11

# Entertainment and Nightlife

## BELLA UNION
bellaunion.com.au
Comedy, theater and music play year-round in the old council chambers at Trades Hall.
⊞ F4 ✉ 54 Victoria Street, Carlton ☎ 9419 5137
🕐 Daily 5.30–11pm 🚋 Tram 1, 3, 5, 6, 8

## CINEMA NOVA
cinemanova.com.au
This art-house cinema complex offers top new-release art-house and commercial films, special film festivals and events. Located in the Lygon Court Shopping Piazza.
⊞ F1 ✉ 380 Lygon Street, Carlton ☎ 9347 5531
🚋 Tram 1, 8

## DAN O'CONNELL HOTEL
thedan.com.au
A warm and welcoming Irish atmosphere and live music seven days a week.
⊞ G1 ✉ 225 Canning Street, Carlton ☎ 9347 1502
🚋 Tram 1, 8, 96

## EVELYN HOTEL
evelynhotel.com.au
This funky hotel has a beer garden, live band music most nights, a front bar with a big screen and pool table—and reasonably priced drinks.
⊞ H1 ✉ 351 Brunswick Street, Fitzroy ☎ 9419 5500
🕐 Daily 🚋 Tram 11

## IMAX
imaxmelbourne.com.au
The screen is the third biggest in the world, the projectors and sound systems are state-of-the-art, and the movies are specially made to suit.
⊞ F3 ✉ Melbourne Museum, Carlton ☎ 9663 5454 🚋 City Circle Tram, 1, 86, 96

## LA MAMA THEATRE
lamama.com.au
One of the city's principal venues for new theater showcases Australian talent.
⊞ F1 ✉ 205 Faraday Street, Carlton ☎ 9347 6948
🚋 Tram 1

## NAKED FOR SATAN
nakedforsatan.com.au
The downstairs bar serves *pintxos* (little bites), vodka, beer and wine. On the roof, via an old lift shaft, is Naked in the Sky, with a bar, lounge, restaurant and terrace

### THE CINEMA SCENE
Melbourne's cinema scene is thriving. Of the many cinemas, the main complexes are at Melbourne Central, the Jam Factory and Crown Entertainment Complex. More alternative cinemas include the Astor in St. Kilda and Kino at Collins Place. For foreign and art-house films try the Cinema Nova in Carlton on Lygon Street. Schedules are online and in *The Age* and *Herald Sun*. The Melbourne International Festival packs out every cinema.

with killer views of Fitzroy and the city.
⊞ H1 ✉ 285 Brunswick Street, Fitzroy ☎ 9416 2238
🕐 Fri–Sat noon–1am, Sun–Thu noon–midnight
🚋 Tram 11

## THE NIGHT CAT
thenightcat.com.au
This popular place spins live funk to world music, plus there's a Sunday salsa dance class.
⊞ H1 ✉ 141 Johnson Street, Fitzroy ☎ 9417 0090
🕐 Wed–Sun 8–1 🚋 Tram 11

## THE PROVINCIAL HOTEL
provincialhotel.com.au
One of Brunswick Street's most popular haunts serves great food, and a huge open fire adds atmosphere and keeps everyone warm in winter.
⊞ H2 ✉ 299 Brunswick Street, Fitzroy ☎ 9810 4193
🕐 Daily 🚋 Tram 11

## RAINBOW HOTEL
therainbow.com.au
Cold beer and great bands are the primary attractions at this hotel.
⊞ H2 ✉ 27 St. David Street, Fitzroy ☎ 9419 4193
🕐 Daily 🚋 Tram 11

## ROYAL PARK
The perfect venue for walking, cycling, tennis, rollerblading and jogging. There are also facilities for golf, football and cricket.
⊞ Off map ✉ Off Royal Parade, Parkville ☎ 9568 9658 🕐 Daily during daylight hours 🚋 Tram 19

# Restaurants

## PRICES

Prices are approximate, based on a 3-course meal for one person.

| | |
|---|---|
| $ | A$20–A$40 |
| $$ | A$41–A$70 |
| $$$ | A$71–A$110 |

### BLUE CHILLIES ($$)

bluechillies.com.au
This stylish Malaysian restaurant serves all the old favorites, including *laksas* and *goreng*.
➕ H2 ✉ 182 Brunswick Street, Fitzroy ☎ 9417 0071 🕐 Mon–Thu 6–10.30pm, Fri–Sat 6–11pm, Sun noon–2.30, 6–10 🚋 Tram 11

### D.O.C. ($$)

docgroup.net
D.O.C. serves great coffee and classic Italian pasta and pizza. There's another branch around the corner.
➕ F1 ✉ 326 Lygon Street, Carlton ☎ 9347 8482 🕐 Mon–Sat 7am–9.30pm, Sun 8am–9pm 🚋 Tram 1

### HOOKED FITZROY ($)

hooked.net.au
Fresh fish and hand-cut chips, plus daily specials are on offer here.
➕ Off map ✉ 384 Brunswick Street, Fitzroy ☎ 9417 7740 🕐 Thu–Sat noon–10, Sun–Wed noon–9.30 🚋 Tram 11

### JIMMY WATSON'S WINE BAR & RESTAURANT ($$)

jimmywatsons.com
This Melbourne institution is the place to socialize and sample wines of great quality. Check out the cellar.
➕ F1 ✉ 333 Lygon Street, Carlton ☎ 9347 3985 🕐 Mon–Sat 11am–late, Sun 4pm–late 🚋 Tram 96

### LEMONGRASS ($$)

lemongrassrestaurant.com.au
Some people call this Melbourne's best Thai restaurant. The food is creative and the setting restrained and elegant. Specializes in ancient royal Thai recipes.
➕ E2 ✉ 174 Lygon Street, Carlton ☎ 9662 2244 🕐 Lunch Mon–Fri, Sun, dinner daily 🚋 Tram 1

### PIREAUS BLUES ($$)

pireausblues.com.au
This Greek restaurant, decorated with tradi-

## THAI AND VIETNAMESE

Australians have turned to Thai food in a big way and the quality of food in the best Thai restaurants in Sydney and Melbourne is equal to that anywhere outside Thailand—light and tasty, based on fresh produce and delicate spices and herbs. Vietnamese cuisine now rivals Thai cuisine in popularity, especially in Melbourne, where many refugees settled after the war in their homeland. Pricey Vietnamese establishments with refined cuisine are proliferating.

tional objects from the homeland, is one of the city's more popular. Reservations essential.
➕ H1 ✉ 310 Brunswick Street, Fitzroy ☎ 9417 0222 🕐 Lunch Wed–Fri and Sun, dinner daily 🚋 Tram 11

### THAI THANI ($$)

thaithani.com.au
Thai Thani is well known for its reasonably priced authentic food, served in faux Thai surroundings.
➕ H1 ✉ 293 Brunswick Street, Fitzroy ☎ 9419 6463 🕐 Dinner daily 🚋 Tram 11

### UNIVERSITY CAFE ($)

This café serves mostly Italian food, and is a great place for a coffee.
➕ E2 ✉ 257 Lygon Street, Carlton ☎ 9347 2142 🕐 Daily 7am–11pm 🚋 Tram 1

### VEGIE BAR ($)

vegiebar.com.au
For over 20 years this busy vegetarian restaurant has been cooking up sensational food that's great for the body and soul.
➕ Off map ✉ 380 Brunswick Street, Fitzroy ☎ 9417 6935 🕐 Mon–Thu 11–10, Fri–Sat 11–10.30, Sun 9am–10pm 🚋 Tram 11

### VIET ROSE ($)

vietrosefitzroy.com.au
Affordable, authentic Vietnamese food is served here. BYO.
➕ Off map ✉ 363 Brunswick Street, Fitzroy ☎ 9417 7415 🕐 Daily 5–10pm 🚋 Tram 11

Try to explore some of the city's outer suburbs and attractions a bit farther out. The city's seaside at St. Kilda is only 20 minutes by tram from the CBD, and a trip on the Great Ocean Road is well worthwhile.

# Heide Museum of Modern Art

Modern buildings and abstract sculpture reflecting the style of art found in the Heide

## THE BASICS

heide.com.au
See map ▷ 93
7 Templestowe Road, Bulleen
Museum: 9850 1500.
Café: 9852 2346
Tue–Sun 10–5
Café
Heidelberg
From station, take bus 903 and alight near the museum
Good
Moderate
Free guided tour at 2pm

## HIGHLIGHTS

● Contemporary art
● Free tour
● Walks
● Sculpture garden
● Heide store

**Celebrating the work of Australia's early modernists, this very special museum and its riverbank sculpture gardens were once the stomping ground of a new generation of artists, whose aim was nothing short of revolutionizing Australian art.**

**The gallery** Set on the banks of the Yarra River, Heide first belonged to John and Sunday Reed, whose patronage, beginning in the 1930s, nurtured a new generation of outstanding artists. Starting with a run-down dairy farm, the Reeds built a fine contemporary home and created an inspiring environment in which artists could meet and work.

**Modern art** Today these buildings house a permanent collection of Australian modernists—paintings by Arthur Boyd, Charles Blackman, Joy Hester, Sidney Nolan, Albert Tucker, Peter Booth and Jenny Watson, and sculptures by Rick Amor and Stephen Killick. The free tour gives insights into the lives of the artists influenced by the Reeds.

**The garden** Stroll around the parklands and picnic in the grounds and along the riverbank. The rambling park comprises native and European trees and has a well-tended kitchen garden and sculpture gardens running right down to the Yarra River. Or try the café at the entrance to the museum. Temporary exhibitions and events offer perspectives on aspects of Australian art.

The Romanesque
Rippon Lea House
(left) and elegant
Como House (right)

## TOP 25

# Rippon Lea House and Como House

**Managed by the National Trust, these outstanding examples of 19th-century suburban estates are just a few kilometers apart, south of the Yarra River. Their magnificent gardens are intact and their architecture is very well preserved.**

**Rippon Lea House** The ornate, Romanesque Rippon Lea House, built in 1868 with distinctive polychome bricks and extended in 1897, has 36 opulent rooms where Victorian splendor mixes with the 1930s tastes of its last owner. The fine 5.7ha (14 acres) Victorian pleasure garden includes an orchard, desert garden, ornamental lake with islands and decorative bridges, a 19th-century conservatory and grand Victorian fernery. Bring a picnic lunch or have a coffee at the Gate House, then spend the afternoon touring the mansion and relaxing by the lake. Access to the house is by tour only, so book ahead.

**Como House** Two hectares (5 acres) of gardens surround this elegant home, built between 1847 and 1859, in an unusual mix of Australian Regency and Italianate styles. This gracious building perfectly exemplifies the wealthy landowner lifestyle in mid-19th-century Australia. The kitchen outbuilding dates from the 1840s, and the original laundry remains. Sloping lawns, walks among flower gardens, and pine and cypress glades make up the grounds; there's also a croquet lawn, a fountain terrace and a water garden by 19th-century landscape designer Ellis Stones.

## THE BASICS

**Rippon Lea House**
ripponleaestate.com.au
➕ See map ▷ 93
✉ 192 Hotham Street, Elsternwick
☎ 9523 6095
🕐 Daily 10–5
🚋 Tram 67
♿ Moderate
❓ Guided tours daily

**Como House**
comohouse.com.au
➕ See map ▷ 93
✉ Corner of Williams Road and Lechlade Avenue, South Yarra
☎ 9827 2500
🕐 2nd and 4th Sat–Sun of month 10–5
🚋 Tram 8
♿ Moderate
❓ Available for group bookings any day

## HIGHLIGHTS

- Unique architecture
- Original furniture
- Park-like grounds
- Fountain terrace
- Stunning interior decoration

**FARTHER AFIELD TOP 25**

95

# Scienceworks

*Hands-on and action packed—the exciting Scienceworks museum caters for all ages*

## THE BASICS

museumvictoria.com.au/
scienceworks/
🔲 See map ▷ 92
✉ 2 Booker Street,
Spotswood
☎ 9392 4800, 13 11 02
🕐 Daily 10–4.30.
Pumping station: daily
for guided tours
🍴 Café
🚉 Spotswood
⛴ Ferry from Southbank
💲 Inexpensive

## HIGHLIGHTS

● Hands-on exhibits
● Planetarium shows
● Temporary exhibits
● Old steam pumps

**This hands-on science and technology museum is an exciting showcase of science past, present and future. For a fast, digital trip around the universe, visit the adjacent Planetarium.**

**Exhibitions** In the "Nitty Gritty Super City" there's a construction zone where you can explore science in the city—pedal a pianola, drive a digger and create your own buildings. At "Sportsworks" you can stretch your mind and your muscles. Try the extreme snowboarding experience and the 3D soccer goalie game. Here you can discover your sporting talents and profile. "Think Ahead" displays hundreds of objects from the past, present and speculative future. High-tech meets hands-on to give a projection of future Earth and its lifestyles.

**Planetarium** A great range of shows at this digital planetarium re-creates the night sky and gives you a close-up look at the moon, the stars and our planets. The Planetarium has a 16m (52ft) domed ceiling, reclining seats, a stereo surround-sound system, and a high-resolution projection system that presents an unforgettable and awe-inspiring astronomical experience.

**The Pumping Station** One of Australia's most important industrial heritage sites, the Pumping Station has giant working steam-driven pumps, now driven by compressed air. These were a key component of the city's first centralized sewerage system.

A stunning aerial view of St. Kilda, with the magical Luna Park at its heart

TOP 25

# St. Kilda and Luna Park

**Take a walk along the Esplanade and pier to work up an appetite for a meal in one of the area's many fine restaurants. For cakes and pastries, a visit to nearby Acland Street is a must.**

**The beach** Since Melbourne's early days people have flocked to this beachside suburb, 6.5km (4 miles) southeast of the city, to enjoy the cool sea breezes off Port Phillip Bay. Late in the 19th century, the wealthy built large houses in the area, away from the heat of the city. The beaches are fine for swimming, although there can be an undertow. Windsurfing is popular.

**The streets** Fitzroy and Acland streets are a mix of retail and dining establishments, lively bars and art galleries. Many of the grand old buildings have been restored and the charm of the place is immense. On Sundays an open-air arts and crafts market along the Esplanade draws huge crowds.

**St. Kilda Pier** This popular pier, erected in 1857, is about 150m (164 yards) from the beach end of Fitzroy Street and two blocks northwest of Luna Park. From the end of the pier you can see the grand sweep of the bay around to Port Melbourne.

**Luna Park** Built in 1912, this St. Kilda institution is one of the oldest amusement parks in the world. The carousel that dates back to the park's earliest days remains a great favorite.

## THE BASICS

**St. Kilda**
stkildamelbourne.com.au
See map ▷ 92
Visitor Information: 132 842
24 hours daily
Tram 3A, 12, 16, 96
Generally good
Free

**Luna Park**
lunapark.com.au
See map ▷ 92
9525 5033
Thu–Fri 7–11pm (summer only); Sat 11–11; Sun 11–8
Food stalls
Trams 16, 96
Moderate–expensive

## HIGHLIGHTS

- Swimming in summer
- Cafés on Fitzroy and Acland streets
- Patisseries
- Walking on the pier or along the beach
- St. Kilda Botanical Gardens
- Nightlife

# More to See

### JEWISH MUSEUM OF AUSTRALIA

jewishmuseum.com.au

Dedicated to the conservation, preservation and exhibition of Jewish heritage, this museum presents the Australian–Jewish experience. State-of-the-art interactive displays explain the Jewish year, belief and ritual.

See map ▷ 92 ✉ 26 Alma Road, St. Kilda ☎ 8534 3600 🕐 Tue–Thu 10–4, Fri 10–3, Sun 10–5 🚋 Tram 3, 67 💰 Inexpensive

### MONTSALVAT

montsalvat.com.au

This amazing group of buildings was handcrafted between 1934 and the 1970s, using mud brick, stone, hewn timbers and slate building materials recycled from some of Melbourne's fine old buildings.

See map ▷ 93 ✉ 7 Hillcrest Avenue, Eltham ☎ 9439 7712 🕐 Daily 9–5 🚆 To Eltham then take 582 bus 💰 Moderate

### RAAF MUSEUM POINT COOK

airforce.gov.au/raafmuseum

Based at Point Cook, the birthplace of the Australian Flying Corps and the Royal Australian Air Force, this museum presents the history of the second-oldest air force in the world.

See map ▷ 92 ✉ RAAF Base Williams, Point Cook Road, Point Cook ☎ 8348 6040 🕐 Tue–Fri 10–3, Sat–Sun 10–5. Interactive flying displays Tue, Thu, Sun 1 🚆 Werribee Park Shuttle daily to Point Cook 💰 Free/donations

### WILLIAMSTOWN

This bayside suburb is best reached by the Westgate Bridge or by a ferry from Southbank and seaside St. Kilda. Shipping docks, moored yachts, boat chandlers and the restored World War II corvette HMAS Castlemaine all contribute to the maritime atmosphere. Walk along the Strand to take in the arts and crafts shops.

See map ▷ 92 ✉ The Strand, The Marina 🍴 Many cafés and restaurants 🚢 Southbank

City ferries at Williamstown

Open-air drinks break in Williamstown
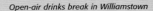

## DANDENONG RANGES

The scenic Dandenongs have always been the favored summer recreation destination for many Melburnians.

Soaring mountain ash forests, glades of tree ferns and mountain streams are all part of the experience in the Dandenongs. The highest point is Mount Dandenong at 633m (2,076ft). Besides hiking and picnicking, there are magnificent gardens, art and craft shops, nurseries and tearooms to visit. Along the southeastern slopes, on the edge of Sherbrooke Forest Park, the narrow-gauge Puffing Billy Railway carries day-trippers from quaint Belgrave, in the foothills, to pretty Emerald Lake Park in the mountains.

William Ricketts Sanctuary, set in a 1.6ha (4-acre) wooded area, displays 200 half-hidden, kiln-fired, clay sculptures of Aboriginal figures, the work of the talented sculptor William Ricketts (1898–1993), who founded the sanctuary, nestled among mossy rocks and tree ferns. Follow the path around the tranquil setting and visit the log cabin Visual Display Centre to watch a short documentary.

### THE BASICS

experiencethedandenongs.com.au
**Distance:** 35km (22 miles) east of the city
**Journey Time:** 45 minutes
ℹ Visitor Centre: 1211 Burwood Highway, Upper Ferntree Gully ☎ 9758 7522 ⏰ Daily 10–4.30
🚉 Ferntree Gully, then Bus 693
♿ Poor
💰 Moderate

## HEALESVILLE SANCTUARY

One of Australia's most highly regarded wildlife parks, Healesville is set in the foothills of the scenic Yarra Valley.

On display are more than 200 native species, including kangaroos, emus, koalas, wombats, dingoes and platypuses in surroundings as near natural as possible. You can learn about the animals from their keepers, as they go on their daily rounds. There are also walk-through aviaries, a wetlands walkway and a nocturnal house. See the working wildlife hospital where sick, injured and orphaned wildlife are cared for, and talk with the vets about native wildlife health. Learn about Australia's majestic birds of prey and parrots at the spectacular Spirits of the Sky show. Tales from Platypus Creek lets you get up close to platypuses. Both events are held daily.

### THE BASICS

zoo.org.au/healesville
**Distance:** 60km (38 miles)
**Journey Time:** 1 hour
✉ Badger Creek Road, Healesville
☎ 5957 2800
⏰ Daily 9–5
🍴 Café; picnic areas
🚌 Bus tour
💰 Expensive

## GREAT OCEAN ROAD

Built by soldiers returned from World War I, and opened in 1932, the Great Ocean Road is one of the world's great scenic drives.

The journey from Torquay, southwest of Melbourne, to Warrnambool and beyond encompasses rain forests, seaside beach towns, cliff-edge roadways, forests and dramatic off-shore rock formations. Past Torquay and nearby Bells Beach (regarded as Australia's surfing capital) is the popular and quaint seaside town of Lorne, and the nearby fishing port Apollo Bay. Near Port Campbell you encounter the famed Twelve Apostles, natural rock formations, weathered by the wind and water, standing in the ocean just offshore. Loch Ard Gorge, the site of a legendary shipwreck, can be reached by a walking trail. The Great Ocean Road is an excellent bus day tour, but could also be undertaken in a more leisurely way as a self-drive trip.

### THE BASICS

visitgreatoceanroad.org.au
**Distance:** 243km (150 miles)
**Journey Time:** 8 hours
🛈 Geelong and Great Ocean Road Visitor Centre
✉ Princes Highway, Little River ☎ 1800 755 611
🚌 Bus tours from Melbourne

## PHILLIP ISLAND

On the island's Summerland Beach you can view a colony of little penguins every night at the Penguin Parade.

Spotlights illuminate these engaging birds as thousands of them return to their nesting burrows in the evening. There is commentary from an experienced ranger and a choice of viewing options, including the Penguin Sky Box, an elevated viewing tower. Bring warm clothing, as nights can be cold and the weather unpredictable. Phillip Island has a substantial waterbird population and there are elevated boardwalks through bushland allowing good viewing opportunities.

At the Koala Conservation Centre, located on Phillip Island Tourist Road in Cowes (tel 5951 2800, daily 10–5, moderate), you can wander along treetop boardwalks and easily spot koalas, or walk the 1km (0.6-mile) track around the center, where there are signs pointing to koalas in trees. Look also for wallabies, echidnas and native birds.

### THE BASICS

visitphillipisland.com
**Distance:** 140km (86 miles)
**Journey Time:** 2 hours
🛈 Phillip Island Visitor Centre ✉ 896 Phillip Island Road, Newhaven ☎ 5956 7447 🕐 Daily 10–two hours after sunset. Penguin Parade every night after sunset
🍴 Restaurants; picnic areas
✋ Moderate to expensive

FARTHER AFIELD EXCURSIONS

## THE BASICS

**Distance:** 29km (18 miles)
**Journey Time:** 45 minutes
✉ The Mansion at Werribee, Open Range Zoo and Victoria State Rose Garden: K Road, Werribee
☎ The Mansion: 8734 5100. Open Range Zoo: 9731 9600, zoo.org.au/werribee
🕐 The Mansion: daily 10–5. Victoria State Rose Garden: daily 9–5. Open Range Zoo: daily 9–5
🍴 Kiosk and bistro
♿ Moderate

## WERRIBEE MANSION AND OPEN RANGE ZOO

This renovated old mansion stands on the banks of the Werribee River, a 30-minute drive from the city, on the way to Geelong.

Here guides in period costume, and audio headphones, show this imposing, 19th-century example of Australia's pastoral heritage to its best advantage. Constructed between 1874 and 1877, the Italianate mansion, with its 10ha (25 acres) of formal grounds, bluestone farm buildings and orchard, is the largest private residence ever built in Victoria. Next to the mansion, the Victoria State Rose Garden has over 5,000 rose bushes.

At the Open Range Zoo you can either stroll around the zoo's 225ha (556 acres) at your own pace, or take a 90-minute guided safari around the grassy plains and sweeping river terraces. Giraffes, zebra, antelope and hippos roam freely here. Walking tracks pass natural enclosures with cheetahs, monkeys and ostriches.

## THE BASICS

experienceyarravalley.com.au
**Distance:** 52km (32 miles) northeast of Melbourne
**Journey Time:** Allow a full day
ℹ Yarra Valley Visitor Information Centre
☎ 5962 2600
**Yarra Valley Dairy**
✉ McMeikans Road, Yering
☎ 9739 0023
**Yarra Valley Wine Tasting Tours**
☎ 9650 0888

## YARRA VALLEY

Northeast of Melbourne, the Yarra River is very different to how it is in the city, and makes for a great day trip.

In the pretty town of Eltham, don't miss the artists' colony at Montsalvat (▷ 98). At Yering, the Yarra Valley Dairy offers handmade cheeses and local cuisine. At the turn of the 20th century, 75 percent of all Australian wines came from Victoria, and the Yarra Valley was one of the most productive wine regions in Australia. Today around 4 percent of the nation's wines are produced in this region and its 80-plus vineyards welcome visitors and sell on their premises.

Farther on is Healesville Sanctuary (▷ 99), with its native animal species, including the rarely seen platypus, in natural surroundings of bushland and wetlands. Many bus tours run to this district.

# Shopping

### A1 LEBANESE BAKERY

a1lebanesebakery.com.au
All the hard-to-get spices, oils and other exotic ingredients are here, plus breads and sweets.
Off map ✉ 643 Sydney Road, Brunswick ☎ 9386 0440 🚋 Tram 19

### ARMADALE ANTIQUE CENTRE

armadaleantiquecentre.com.au
Quality antiques and collectibles are sold in this center at the heart of popular Armadale high street's antique area.
Off map ✉ 1147 High Street, Armadale ☎ 9822 7788 🕐 Daily 10–5 🚋 Tram 6

### CAMBERWELL SUNDAY MARKET

sundaymarket.com.au
Several hundred stall-holders sell a wide assortment of bric-a-brac.
Off map ✉ Station Street, Camberwell 🕐 Sun 7am–12.30pm 🚋 Tram 70, 72, 75

### CAMPBELLFIELD TRASH AND TREASURE MARKET

Everything imaginable is for sale, but you'll need a taxi to get here.
Off map ✉ Hume Resource Centre, Bolinda Road, Campbellfield ☎ 0409 450 734 🕐 Sat 8–2

### DE BORTOLI WINERY AND RESTAURANT

debortoliyarra.com.au
This is one of the best wineries and restaurants in the Yarra Valley, with fantastic views. Sample, then buy your wines, pick up some great cheeses and dine on the excellent northern Italian food based on local produce. You need a car to get here.
Off map ✉ 58 Pinnacle Lane, Dixons Creek ☎ 5965 2271

### MATCHBOX

matchbox.com.au
Long-established gift shop, specializing in design and new concepts and trends.
Off map ✉ 1055 High Street, Armadale ☎ 9821 0691 🚋 Tram 6

### NATIONAL WOOL MUSEUM SHOP

geelongaustralia.com.au/nwm
An excellent range of wool products is for sale at Australia's only comprehensive wool museum, in a century-old wool store and featuring displays and hands-on exhibits highlighting all facets of this industry.

---

## MEGA MALLS

A trip to Melbourne's major suburban shopping centers provides a chance to mingle with the locals in their own environment. You'll find cinemas, restaurants and free entertainment. Try the Chadstone Shopping Centre (✉ 1341 Dandenong Road, Chadstone 🕐 Mon–Wed, 9–5.30, Thu–Fri 9–9, Sat 9–5, Sun 10–5).

---

Off map ✉ 26 Moorabool Street, Geelong ☎ 5272 4701 🕐 Daily 9–5

### PHILLIPPA'S BAKERY PROVISIONS

phillipas.com.au
There's not much room to eat in here, but the huge selection of breads, cakes and other produce can yield a tasty take-away lunch or picnic.
Off map ✉ 1030 High Street, Armadale ☎ 9576 2020 🚋 Tram 6

### ST. KILDA

Melbourne's most vibrant suburb combines beachside frivolity with serious dining, great shopping and a Sunday arts and crafts market (▷ 97 and below). Fitzroy Street and Acland Street are essential stops.
Off map ✉ Fitzroy and Acland streets, St. Kilda 🚋 Tram 16, 96

### ST. KILDA ESPLANADE MARKET

stkildaesplanademarket.com.au
Original works made by stallholders at this popular Sunday arts and crafts market draw shoppers from far and wide.
Off map ✉ The Upper Esplanade, St. Kilda 🕐 Sun 10–4 🚋 Tram 16, 96

### WILLIAMSTOWN

This waterfront village is full of arts and crafts stalls, antiques stores and coffee shops.
Off map ✉ The Strand, Williamstown 🚉 Williamstown

# Entertainment and Nightlife

## ABSOLUTE OUTDOORS

absoluteoutdoors.com.au
Try your hand at abseiling, take a challenging mountain-bike ride and finish with a tranquil canoe tour in the spectacular Grampians National Park.
➕ Off map ✉ 105 Main Road, Halls Gap ☎ 5356 4556 🕒 Daily tours

## BALLOONMAN

balloonman.com.au
View Melbourne from a hot-air balloon followed by a champagne breakfast.
➕ Off map ✉ 10 Bond Street, Abbotsford ☎ 9427 0088 🕒 Daily at dawn

## CLIFFHANGER CLIMBING GYM

cliffhanger.com.au
Australia's tallest indoor rock climbing facility has walls ranging from 6m (20ft) to 20m (66ft) tall.
➕ Off map ✉ Grieve Parade, Altona North ☎ 9369 6400 🕒 Daily

## DINNER PLAIN TRAIL RIDES

highcountryhorserides.com.au
Based in the Dinner Plain Valley, near Mt. Hotham, this company offers one-day and multiday riding trips into remote alpine areas.
➕ Off map ✉ PO Box 36, Dinner Plain ☎ 1300 855 907 🕒 Rides on demand

## THE ESPLANADE

espy.com.au
On weekends, local music lovers pack this St. Kilda institution, a legend among those who love live music. You can have a meal in the restaurant or watch the sunset.
➕ Off map ✉ 11 The Esplanade, St. Kilda ☎ 9534 0211 🕒 Daily 🚊 Tram 16

## FLEMINGTON RACECOURSE

flemington.com.au
This racecourse hosts the Melbourne Cup and has a regular program of race days year-round.
➕ Off map ✉ 448 Epsom Road, Flemington ☎ 1300 727 575 🚊 Tram 57

## MERIDIAN KAYAK ADVENTURES

meridienkayak.com.au
Explore the sea at close quarters along Victoria's spectacular coast: Wilsons Promontory, Cape Otway, the Twelve Apostles.

### WATER SPORTS

Melbourne's location on Port Phillip Bay provides great opportunities for water sports. You can surf at Mornington Peninsula and near Flinders, windsurf from Sandringham (☎ 9598 2867), go diving in the bay (☎ 9459 4111), or sail with the Yachtmaster Sailing School (☎ 9699 9425). Swim at the bayside beaches close to Melbourne, between Port Melbourne and St. Kilda, and from St. Kilda to Portsea, and in the many public pools.

➕ Off map ✉ 40A Bardia Avenue, Seaford ☎ 9786 0987 🕒 Tours on demand

## MOONRAKER DOLPHIN SWIMS

moonrakercharters.com.au
On boat tours in pristine Port Phillip Bay, you may choose to swim with the wild dolphins or simply sightsee in comfort.
➕ Off map ✉ Esplanade Road, Sorrento ☎ 5984 4211 🕒 Tours on demand

## THE PRINCE BAND ROOM

princebandroom.com.au
A hot-spot venue for top musicians, with quality club gear and lighting.
➕ Off map ✉ 29 Fitzroy Street, St. Kilda ☎ 9536 1168 🕒 Daily, usually from 8pm 🚊 Tram 16, 96

## RIVIERA NAUTIC

rivieranautic.com.au
Sail the Gippsland Lakes to a variety of destinations on a choice of yachts; equipment provided.
➕ Off map ✉ Chinamans Creek, Metung ☎ 5156 2243 🕒 On demand

## ST. KILDA SEA BATHS

stkildaseabaths.com.au
Near St. Kilda Pier, the complex houses a 25m public pool, gym facilities and spa, plus cafés and restaurants.
➕ Off map ✉ 10–18 Jacka Boulevard, St. Kilda ☎ 9525 4888 🕒 Mon–Thu 5am–11pm, Fri 5am–10pm, Sat 7am–8pm, Sun 8–8 🚊 Tram 16, 96

FARTHER AFIELD   ENTERTAINMENT AND NIGHTLIFE

# Restaurants

## PRICES

Prices are approximate, based on a 3-course meal for one person.

| | |
|---|---|
| $ | A$20–A$40 |
| $$ | A$41–A$70 |
| $$$ | A$71–A$110 |

## CIRCA ($$$)

circa.com.au

Circa has achieved near perfection with its attention to detail, discreet service, elegant setting and innovative Modern Australian food. Pricey.

Off map ✉ 2 Acland Street, St. Kilda ☎ 9536 1122 🕐 Lunch and dinner daily 🚃 Tram 16, 96

## DONOVANS ($$$)

donovanshouse.com.au

This favorite, in a good beachside location, serves Mediterranean dishes with a modern twist.

Off map ✉ 40 Jacka Boulevard, St. Kilda ☎ 9534 8221 🕐 Lunch Mon–Fri, dinner daily 🚃 Tram 16, 96

## HARRY'S KIOSK ($)

Sit outside near the water at Queenscliff, and enjoy fresh seafood and simple brunch fare. Car needed.

Off map ✉ 1 Tobin Street, Queenscliff ☎ 5258 3750 🕐 Breakfast and lunch daily

## THE HEALESVILLE HOTEL ($$)

healesvillehotel.com.au

This country pub has a contemporary menu and an interesting wine list.

Off map ✉ 256 Maroondah Highway, Healesville ☎ 5962 4002 🕐 Lunch and dinner daily

## PORTSEA HOTEL ($$)

portseahotel.com.au

Enjoy alfresco dining with classic hotel fare and stunning views of Port Phillip Bay.

Off map ✉ 3746 Point Nepean Road, Portsea ☎ 5984 2213 🕐 Lunch and dinner daily

## SAILS ON THE BAY ($$$)

sailsonthebay.com.au

Fresh seafood is the specialty of this waterfront restaurant, with fine views day and night.

Off map ✉ 15 Elwood Foreshore, Elwood ☎ 9525 6933 🕐 Lunch and dinner Tue–Sat 🚃 Tram 1

## SEAFOOD

Seafood is popular in this bayside city. Local specialties include Melbourne rock oysters, Tasmanian scallops, kingfish, prawns, smoked salmon and South Australian tuna. Northern fish such as barramundi grace menus all over town. Appropriately, many seafood restaurants have waterfront locations, where you can buy excellent fish and chips to go—St. Kilda, Brighton and Williamstown are particularly good spots for alfresco eating.

## SAPORE ($$$)

sapore.com.au

This trendy restaurant serves modern Italian food in a bold, streamlined setting. Classic desserts and good value.

Off map ✉ 3 Fitzroy Street, St. Kilda ☎ 9534 9666 🕐 Lunch and dinner daily 🚃 Tram 16, 96

## SKY HIGH RESTAURANT ($$)

skyhighmtdandenong.com. au/dining

Contemporary Australian dining with sensational observatory views of the Mornington Peninsula to Port Phillip Bay.

Off map ✉ 26 Observatory Road, Mount Dandenong ☎ 9751 0452 🕐 Lunch and dinner daily; booking essential

## VUE GRAND HOTEL ($$)

vuegrand.com.au

Choose from a menu of fine cuisine and a great craft beer and wine list in this majestic grand dining room.

Off map ✉ 46 Hesse Street, Queenscliff ☎ 5258 1544 🕐 Dinner Wed–Sat; booking essential

## WILD OAK CAFÉ ($$)

wildoak.com.au

Enjoy seasonal Modern Australian cuisine and a great wine list in this relaxed dining setting.

Off map ✉ 232 Ridge Road, Olinda ☎ 9751 2033 🕐 Lunch and dinner Wed–Sun

Melbourne offers every category of accommodations, from basic budget hotels to luxurious properties with the latest amenities.

# Introduction

Take your pick from a range of areas to stay, in all types of accommodation. You may prefer the quieter suburbs to the buzz of central Melbourne.

### A Wide Choice

Melbourne has plenty of accommodation options. At the upper end there's the luxurious Westin (▷ 112) and the Stamford Plaza (▷ 112), and the less expensive, classy boutique The Prince (▷ 111) at St. Kilda. At the lower end are the comfortable rooms at The Nunnery and the convenient Hotel Claremont. There are also many economical, self-catering apartments and reasonably priced guesthouses, and hostels are plentiful. Bed-and-breakfasts are numerous, especially in outer suburbs and rural areas close to the city.

### Where to Stay

Melbourne's major hotel areas are located around the city center, East Melbourne, North Melbourne and Southbank. Most hotels have in-room Internet connections or wireless areas for laptops.

### Get a Bargain

It's worth looking on the Internet for special deals, for both advance bookings and last-minute rate reductions. But be aware that there are popular times of the year, such as around Melbourne Cup time (early November) and the Grand Prix (mid-March), when hotels are fully booked, so advance reservations are essential.

#### STAY AT THE AIRPORT

Although Melbourne's CBD is only 22km (14 miles) from the international airport, there are times when a stay at an airport hotel is necessary. There are three good options, one in each of the price ranges: budget, mid-range and luxury. Ibis Budget Melbourne Airport (☎ 8336 1811) is a good budget option; Holiday Inn Melbourne Airport offers mid-range value (☎ 9933 5111); ParkRoyal Melbourne Airport (☎ 8347 2000) is the top-end choice.

# Budget Hotels

## 169 DRUMMOND STREET

169drummond.com.au

This gay-friendly bed-and-breakfast is close to the shops and restaurants of Lygon Street in Carlton and has king, queen and twin rooms, laundry facilities and a garden area.

⊞ F2 ⊠ 169 Drummond Street, Carlton ☎ 9663 3081 🚋 Tram 1, 3, 5, 6, 8

## CITY CENTRE BUDGET HOTEL

citycentrebudgethotel.com.au

City Centre is one of the best hotels in this price range, with wireless Internet, shared bathrooms and rooftop deck.

⊞ G5 ⊠ 22–30 Little Collins Street ☎ 9654 5401 🚋 City Circle Tram

## CITY LIMITS

citylimitscom.au

Just on the edge of Chinatown and a minute from the CBD, this quiet hotel has free WiFi, Foxtel and breakfast.

⊞ G4 ⊠ 20–22 Little Bourke Street ☎ 9662 2544 🚋 Tram 86, 96

## CREST ON BARKLY

crestob.com.au

At the top of St. Kilda, Crest on Barkly is a 20-minute walk from the beach or a 10-minute tram ride into the city. The hotel's budget standard rooms have all the creature comforts, plus a fitness center and guest laundry.

⊞ Off map ⊠ 47 Barkly Street, St. Kilda ☎ 9537 1788 🚋 Tram 3, 3A, 16, 67

## THE GREAT SOUTHERN HOTEL

greatsouthernhotel.com.au

Comfortable and affordable, this hotel has two types of accommodations suitable for both business and budget travelers.

⊞ C7 ⊠ 44 Spencer Street ☎ 9329 2552 🚋 Any Flinders Street tram

## HOTEL CLAREMONT GUESTHOUSE

hotelclaremont.com

The Claremont is a great value, convenient guesthouse with communal facilities and bright rooms.

⊞ Off map ⊠ 189 Toorak Road, South Yarra ☎ 9826 8000 🚋 Tram 8

## JASPER HOTEL

jasperhotel.com.au

This hotel offers a good range of reasonably priced accommodation, plus a fitness center, an indoor pool and café.

⊞ D4 ⊠ 489 Elizabeth Street ☎ 1800 468 359 🚋 City Circle Tram

## THE NUNNERY

nunnery.com.au

Clean, centrally-heated rooms, comfortable communal facilities, and a great atmosphere ensure that this place remains popular with budget travelers.

⊞ Off map ⊠ 116 Nicholson Street, Fitzroy ☎ 9419 8637 🚋 Tram 96

## PENSIONE HOTEL

pensione.com.au

Close to Southbank and Southern Cross Station, Pensione Hotel is a modern hotel with a restaurant, bar and rooftop sundeck. With matchbox- and shoebox-themed rooms, it caters to the budget traveler.

⊞ C7 ⊠ 16 Spencer Street ☎ 9621 3333 🚋 Any Flinders Street tram

## SPACE HOTEL

spacehotel.au

Facilities at this comfortable hotel with dorms, family and private rooms, include a gym, movie room, Internet café, shared kitchen and a rooftop sundeck with spa.

⊞ E4 ⊠ 380 Russell Street ☎ 9662 3888 🚋 Tram 24, 30, 35

## TUNE HOTEL

tunehotels.com/au/en/our-hotels/melbourne/

This large modern hotel is just two tram stops from the CBD. The comfortable rooms have power showers. A buy-on package is required for towels, pay TV, toiletries and WiFi.

⊞ E3 ⊠ 609 Swanston Street, Carlton ☎ 9347 3027 🚋 Tram 1, 3, 5, 6, 8

# Mid-Range Hotels

## PRICES

Expect to pay between A$150 and A$250 per night for a double room in a mid-range hotel.

### ADINA APARTMENT HOTEL

tfehotels.com/brands/adina-apartment-hotels
Located right at the heart of Melbourne's attractions, the Adina is convenient for the Royal Botanic Gardens, Rod Laver Arena and the Yarra River. There are well-maintained kitchens, gym and on-site parking. No restaurant, but there is a delivery service available.
➕ G6 ✉ 88 Flinders Street ☎ 8663 0000 🚋 Tram 48, 70, 75

### ATLANTIS HOTEL

atlantishotel.com.au
Situated near most major attractions, theaters and department stores, this stylish hotel has suites with great views over the city and Victoria Harbour.
➕ B5 ✉ 300 Spencer Street ☎ 9600 2900 🚋 Tram 86

### BATMAN'S HILL ON COLLINS

batmanshill.com.au
This hotel is just a few minutes' stroll from the Crown Entertainment Complex, the Yarra River and Southern Cross Station.
➕ C7 ✉ 623 Collins Street ☎ 9614 6344 🚉 Southern Cross

### COSMOPOLITAN HOTEL

cosmopolitanhotel.com.au
The Cosmopolitan is a modern boutique hotel with 88 rooms in the heart of St. Kilda. There's a café on-site, as well as free WiFi and parking.
➕ Off map ✉ 2–8 Carlisle Street, St. Kilda ☎ 9534 0781 🚋 Tram 3A, 16, 79

### THE CULLEN

artserieshotels.com.au/cullen
Adam Cullen's original artworks adorn the walls of this boutique hotel. It's a short tram ride from the city center and is located beside some of Melbourne's hippest bars and restaurants. Accommodation is spacious and rooms at the top have fabulous views of the city.
➕ Off map ✉ 164 Commercial Road, Prahran ☎ 9098 1555 🚋 Tram 72

## COUNTRY STYLE

Be sure to experience the green splendor of the Dandenong Ranges, an hour east of the city center. One of the best places to stay here is Arcadia Cottages (✉ 188 Falls Road, Olinda ☎ 9751 1017, arcardiacottages.com.au). These superbly furnished and individually crafted cottages are set in an attractive garden and include hot tubs and wood-fired heaters. Reservations recommended.

### DOWNTOWNER ON LYGON

downtowner.com.au
Within easy walking distance of the city, the Queen Victoria Market and the varied restaurants of Lygon Street, this friendly hotel is of a very high standard.
➕ E3 ✉ 66 Lygon Street ☎ 9663 5555 🚋 City Circle Tram

### HOTEL CAUSEWAY

causeway.com.au
Surrounded by boutiques and eateries, this conveniently located hotel offers business and fitness centers, and a delicious buffet breakfast.
➕ E6 ✉ 275 Little Collins Street ☎ 9660 8888 🚋 Any Swanston Street tram

### HOTEL GRAND CHANCELLOR

grandchancellorhotels.com/au/melbourne/
This comfortable hotel in the heart of the city, with Chinatown and the theater district on its doorstep, has the feel of a place with much more expensive rates.
➕ F5 ✉ 131 Lonsdale Street ☎ 9656 4000 🚋 City Circle Tram

### KINGSGATE HOTEL

kingsgatehotel.com.au
Within walking distance of many attractions, this friendly hotel has spacious rooms, with all the usual amenities, plus an on-site restaurant and bar.

✚ C6  ✉ 131 King Street
☎ 9629 4171  🚋 Tram
86, 96

## MAGNOLIA COURT HOTEL

magnolia-court.com.au
This family-run hotel with
its own terrace café is in
a peaceful and prestig-
ious setting amid leafy
historic houses. Rooms
range from a luxury self-
contained apartment to
compact units.
✚ J5  ✉ 101 Powlett Street,
East Melbourne  ☎ 9419
4222  🚋 Tram 48, 75 from
Flinders Street

## MECURE WELCOME HOTEL

mecurewelcome.com.au
In a handy location, right
in the center of the city
and close to the major
department stores and
the CBD, this popular
hotel has great facilities,
all at a very reasonable
price.
✚ E5  ✉ 265 Little Bourke
Street  ☎ 9639 0555  🚋 City
Circle Tram

## OAKS ON COLLINS

oakshotelresorts.com
This comfortable
apartment hotel is
conveniently situated in
the CBD near Southgate
and the Crown Casino.
It has New York-style
studio apartments, a res-
taurant and lounge bar,
10m (33ft) lap pool, gym
and sauna.
✚ E6  ✉ 480 Collins Street
☎ 1300 786 603  🚋 Tram
11, 12, 109

## PARKVIEW ST. KILDA ROAD HOTEL

viewhotels.com.au
Located not far from
the city, Parkview has
well appointed rooms,
a restaurant and bar,
roof-top spa and sauna,
and is close to the shop-
ping and attractions in
St. Kilda, Southbank and
the CBD.
✚ Off map  ✉ 562 St.
Kilda Road  ☎ 9529 8888
🚋 Tram 3, 5, 6, 64, 67, 72

## THE PRINCE

theprince.com.au
Nothing quite matches
a stay at this particularly
stylish and elegant bou-
tique hotel. With private
bay-view balcony suites,
it's the home of one of
the city's top restaurants,
Circa (▷ 106).
✚ Off map  ✉ 2 Acland
Street, St. Kilda  ☎ 9536
1111  🚋 Tram 16

## APARTMENTS

Renting quarters in one of
Melbourne's apartment-
style hotels generally falls
into the moderate price
range. Many of these apartments, with full maid service, are large enough for
families or small groups.
They have from one to
three bedrooms, with
separate dining areas and
kitchens or kitchenettes.
One of the best of these
is The Mantra on Russell
(✉ 222 Russell Street
☎ 9915 2500) in the CBD.

## RADISSON ON FLAGSTAFF GARDENS

radisson.com
The reliable Radisson
is conveniently located
in the heart of the city,
opposite historic Flagstaff
Gardens. This 184-room
hotel has a health and
fitness center, a business
center, nonsmoking floors
and convenient valet
parking.
✚ C5  ✉ 380 William Street
☎ 9322 8000  🚋 City Circle
Tram

## TOLARNO HOTEL

tolarnohotel.com.au
This boutique hotel is
in a heritage building in
the heart of St. Kilda. All
rooms are en suite and
feature original artwork.
View the fabulous art
collection and dine on
classic European fare at
the hotel restaurant.
✚ Off map  ✉ 42 Fitzroy
Street, St. Kilda  ☎ 9537 0200
🚋 Tram 3A, 16, 96

## TRAVELODGE HOTEL SOUTHBANK

tfehotels.com
Within easy walking
distance of the aquarium,
art galleries, the Crown
Casino, Royal Botanic
Gardens and the
Melbourne Exhibition
Centre. Air-conditioned
rooms, all amenities, and
a local restaurant will
deliver right to your room.
✚ E7  ✉ 9 Riverside Quay,
Southbank (a short walk
across the bridge from Flinders
Street Station)  ☎ 8696 9600
🚇 Flinders Street

# Luxury Hotels

## PRICES

Expect to pay over A$250 per night for a double room at a luxury hotel.

### THE COMO
accorhotels.com
This top hotel, located in the vibrant heart of South Yarra, has studios and suites, great food, a gymnasium, sauna and pool. It's close to some of Melbourne's most popular shops, bars and restaurants.
Off map ☒ 630 Chapel Street, South Yarra ☎ 9825 2222 🚋 Tram 78, 79

### CROWN PROMENADE
crownpromenade.com.au
The ultimate in luxury, this hotel has a casino, world-class health center, classy shopping centers and stylish waterfront restaurants at its doorstep. Treat youself to something special.
E7 ☒ Southbank ☎ 9292 6688 🚋 Flinders Street 🚋 Tram 12, 96, 109

### GRAND HYATT MELBOURNE
melbourne.grand.hyatt.com
One of Melbourne's best hotels, the Grand Hyatt has very good restaurants, a health and fitness center, first-class business facilities and exclusive boutiques.
F6 ☒ 123 Collins Street ☎ 9657 1234 🚋 City Circle Tram

### INTERCONTINENTAL MELBOURNE RIALTO
melbourne.intercontinental.com
Stylish luxury hotel in a heritage-listed building, with top service, a great location next to the Rialto Towers, bars, a brasserie and a heated rooftop pool and sauna.
D7 ☒ 495 Collins Street ☎ 8627 1400 🚋 City Circle Tram

### LANGHAM HOTEL
langhamhotels.com.au
Close to the Arts Centre action and the Crown Entertainment Complex, this top hotel has a business center, a health club and a heated pool.
E7 ☒ 1 Southgate Avenue (short walk from city center) ☎ 8696 8888

## DAY SPAS

Many of Melbourne's hotels have put aside areas to cater for this popular form of indulgence, where you can renew the body, mind and soul and leave revitalized and refreshed. Treatments include facials, several different types of massage, including remedial and deep tissue, and practitioners in naturopathy, acupuncture and aromatherapy may be on hand. Good choices include the Park Club Health and Day Spa at the Park Hyatt Melbourne (▷ this page) and Aurora Spa at The Prince (▷ 111).

### PARK HYATT MELBOURNE
melbourne.park.hyatt.com
This luxury hotel provides a warm, distinctive ambience and good service.
Off map ☒ 1 Parliament Square ☎ 9224 1234 🚋 City Circle Tram

### STAMFORD PLAZA
stamford.com.au/spm
This all-suite hotel is within walking distance of a host of Melbourne's attractions, theaters, cinemas and the exclusive end of Collins Street.
F5 ☒ 111 Little Collins Street ☎ 9659 1000 🚋 City Circle Tram

### WESTIN
westin.com.au
Centrally located within the business and entertainment district, this five-star hotel has spacious rooms and suites, superb amenities, and Allegro, one of the city's best restaurants.
F6 ☒ 205 Collins Street ☎ 9635 2222 🚋 City Circle Tram

### WINDSOR HOTEL
thehotelwindsor.com.au
One of the world's finest hotels and certainly Australia's grandest and most steeped in history, this luxury hotel offers fine service and a sense of style. Even if you don't stay here, it's worth checking it out.
G5 ☒ 111 Spring Street ☎ 9633 6000 🚋 City Circle Tram

The more you plan your trip, the more you'll get out of your time in Melbourne, which has so much to offer. These pages of travel advice and facts will give you insider knowledge of the city.

# Planning Ahead

## When to Go

Summer is the busiest and hottest time to visit Melbourne, when festivals and celebrations are happening all over the city, plus it's a good time for a trip to the beach or walks in Melbourne's many beautiful parks and gardens. Be sure to prebook accommodation in busy periods.

### TIME

Daylight Saving operates from the first Sunday in October to the first Sunday in April (11 hours ahead of GMT).

### AVERAGE DAILY MAXIMUM TEMPERATURES

| JAN | FEB | MAR | APR | MAY | JUN | JUL | AUG | SEP | OCT | NOV | DEC |
|-----|-----|-----|-----|-----|-----|-----|-----|-----|-----|-----|-----|
| 79°F | 79°F | 75°F | 68°F | 63°F | 57°F | 55°F | 59°F | 63°F | 68°F | 72°F | 75°F |
| 26°C | 26°C | 24°C | 20°C | 17°C | 14°C | 13°C | 15°C | 17°C | 20°C | 22°C | 24°C |

Melbourne's weather changes frequently—always carry an umbrella, even if it doesn't look like rain. The city enjoys a generally temperate climate.

**Spring** (September–November) is cool to mild, with average highs of 20°C and average lows of 10°C, perfect for being out and about.

**Summer** (December–February) can be warm to hot, and many locals head for the beaches.

**Autumn** (March–May) is mild—good weather for parks and gardens.

**Winter** (June–August) can be wet and cool.

### WHAT'S ON

**January** *Cricket matches:* At the famous Melbourne Cricket Ground.
*Australian Open Tennis:* The classic tournament is at Melbourne Park.

**February** *Chinese New Year:* Two weeks of festivities.

**March** *Formula 1 Australian Grand Prix:* Albert Park.
*The Moomba Festival:* A Melbourne cultural institution that includes parades and exhibitions.
*Melbourne Food and Wine Festival:* Sample Australia's best food and wines here.

**April** *Melbourne International Flower and Garden Show:* Indoor exhibition of plants and garden products.
*Melbourne International Comedy Festival:* One of the largest comedy festivals in the world.
*Rip Curl Pro Classic:* Australia's most prestigious surfing event is held at Torquay.

**May** *Antiques Fair:* The state's premier antiques fair.

**August** *Melbourne International Film Festival:* A showcase for top local and international movies.

**September** *Australian Rules Grand Final:* The city comes to a halt as the top teams compete.
*Royal Melbourne Show:* Eleven days of animals, events, food, art and crafts.

**October/November** *Melbourne Cup and the Spring Racing Carnival:* The Melbourne Cup is the highlight of this series of prestigious races.
*Melbourne Festival:* Art exhibitions, concerts, plays and dance performances.

**December** *New Year's Eve:* Fireworks and partying.

SPIRIT OF TASMANIA

## Melbourne Online

Most hotels in Melbourne will have Internet access in the rooms, an area with wireless connections for laptops or an online computer set up in the lobby.

### melbourne.vic.gov.au
Melbourne's government website for tourists has up-to-date, comprehensive information on city attractions, events, guided tours, shopping, accommodation, eating out and lots more.

### visitmelbourne.com
Melbourne's official travel and accommodation website, with special interest categories such as families, students, gays and lesbians, disabled travelers and backpackers.

### thatsmelbourne.com.au
City of Melbourne website with information on events, things to see and do, shopping, eating, arts and culture, services, maps and transport.

### bom.gov.au
The national bureau of meteorology, with comprehensive weather information and forecasts.

### theage.com.au
*The Age* is Melbourne's major daily newspaper, with coverage of the latest local, national and world news stories, as well as sections on breaking news and business, travel, technology and entertainment.

### smartraveller.com.au
The Australian Government travel advisory service. As well as travel alerts, the site allows you to register your particulars so that you can be contacted in an emergency. It links to sites providing information on travel insurance, health insurance and cheap airline flights.

### samesame.com.au/whatson/melbourne
Australia's gay and lesbian website has a comprehensive guide to events around the city.

## TRAVEL SITES

### ptv.vic.gov.au
For train, tram and bus information, timetables, maps of stations and stops, fares, tickets and a journey planner.

### melbourneairport.com.au
Information on arrival and departure times, shopping and eating, Duty Free shops, facilities and services, and an airport map.

### fodors.com
A complete travel-planning site. You can research prices and weather; reserve air tickets, cars and rooms; pose questions to (and get answers from) fellow visitors; and find links to other sites.

# Getting There

## WHAT TO PACK

● In summer (December–February) the temperature averages 25°C (77°F). Take cotton clothing, a broad-brimmed hat, sunscreen, sunglasses and other summer-weight items, plus an umbrella.

● In winter (June–August) take a raincoat and/or medium-weight coat, plus clothing suitable for an average 13°C (55°F).

## BEFORE YOU GO

● All visitors require a valid passport and an ETA (Electronic Travel Authority). It is fully electronic and is available through travel agents.

● A Tourist ETA is valid for one year (or until the expiry date of your passport, if less), allows for multiple entry and will allow you to stay for a total of three months. Australia does not allow entry if your passport expires within six months of your entry date.

● Vaccination certificates are not normally required, unless you have traveled to an infected country within the previous 14 days.

● Australian Tourist Commission office: Gemini House, Putney Hill, London SW15 ☎ Administration only: 020 8780 2229.

## AIRPORTS

Melbourne Airport is 22km (14 miles) northwest of Melbourne's Central Business District (CBD). Avalon Airport is 50km (31 miles) southwest of central Melbourne.

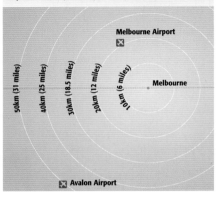

## ARRIVING BY AIR

Melbourne Airport (melbourneairport. com.au) at Tullarmarine, to the north of the city, is the main point of entry for overseas visitors on direct flights. The airport also handles the majority of domestic passenger arrivals. There are taxis and inexpensive bus services, including Skybus (tel 9335 2811, skybus.com.au), that travel into the city, as well as a variety of car rental outlets. A second airport, southwest of the city, Avalon Airport, serves domestic carrier JetStar's flights, and the Sita Coaches (tel 9689 7999) meet flights and take 50 minutes to Melbourne CBD.

## ARRIVING BY SEA

Not the most common means by which to arrive in Melbourne, but the city is an increasingly popular port for cruise liners. Melbourne's Station Pier, 4km (2.5 miles) from the city, serves cruise ships as well as being the dock of the *Spirit of Tasmania* (tel 1800 634 906, spiritoftasmania.com.au), the car and passenger ferry service between Melbourne and Devonport in Tasmania. A tram runs to and

SPIRIT OF TASMANIA

from the pier to Collins Street in the city approximately every 15 minutes.

### ARRIVING BY BUS
Bus travel is often more expensive than flying, but buses are nevertheless one of the best ways to see more of Australia and Victoria on your way to Melbourne. Country and interstate buses pick up and depart from Southern Cross Station. Day and overnight buses arrive each day from Adelaide and Sydney and usually take between 11 and 12 hours. The main interstate carrier is Greyhound Australia (tel 1300 473 946, greyhound.com.au).

### ARRIVING BY TRAIN
Country and interstate trains (tel 9619 2727, vline.com.au) travel to and around Victoria and offer a comfortable, if slower, way to see the state and other parts of Australia. Vline trains arrive at Southern Cross Station, part of the metropolitan train system's underground City Loop service. Countrylink XPT train services (tel 13 22 32, nswtrainlink.info) from Sydney to Melbourne takes around 10–11 hours.

### ARRIVING BY CAR
Car rental is inexpensive in Australia and is a popular way for families to save money on inter-capital travel. The main highways between cities are excellent. Melbourne and larger regional centers have several car rental firms, offering a variety of vehicles and deals. You must be at least 21 years old, and you can pay additional fees to have the insurance excess waived. The main rental companies are Avis, Budget, Europcar, Hertz and Thrifty. Remember there are great distances involved in driving between Australian state capitals and to the many isolated attractions, so good planning is essential for a successful driving holiday. And driving in outback locations requires extra precautions and good driving skills. Check the Australian Automobile Association (aaa.asn.au) for more details.

## CUSTOMS REGULATIONS

● Visitors aged 18 or over may bring in 50 cigarettes or 50g of tobacco or cigars; 2.25l of alcoholic spirits; plus other dutiable goods to the value of A$900 per person.
● There is no limit on money imported for personal use, although amounts in excess of A$10,000 or its equivalent must be declared on arrival.
● The smuggling of all drugs is treated harshly in Australia, and the importing of firearms and items such as ivory or other products from endangered species is illegal or restricted.

## EMERGENCY TELEPHONE NUMBERS

**Police, Ambulance, Fire**
☎ 000 (24 hours)
Calls are free.

## POLICE

The non-emergency police number is ☎ 9247 6666.

## CONSULATES

● **Spain** ✉ 146 Elgin Street, Carlton ☎ 9347 1966
● **UK** ✉ Level 17, 90 Collins Street ☎ 9652 1600
● **US** ✉ 553 St. Kilda Road ☎ 9526 5900

# Getting Around

## PUBLIC TRANSPORT

● Myki cards allow for travel on trams, trains and buses. Three fare zones apply. There's a Free Tram Zone in the CBD that's clearly marked at each tram stop. Zone 1 covers inner Melbourne and Zone 2 outer Melbourne. Check out ptv.vic.gov.au/tickets/zones/ for more information.

● A two-hour full fare in Zone 1 costs up to A$3.75, daily full fare up to A$7.50. Go to ptv.vic.gov.au/tickets/metropolitan-myki-fares/ for up-to-date fare information.

● Myki cards can be bought at the airport, rail and bus stations, and at retail outlets displaying the myki sign. If in doubt call Public Transport Victoria on 1800 800 007.

● Melbourne is unforgiving when it comes to not having a myki card—fines are on-the-spot.

## FEMALE TRAVELERS

Melbourne is generally a safe place for women travelers. However, walking alone in parks or on beaches at night, and traveling alone on out-of-city-center trains at night, is not recommended.

## TRAMS AND LIGHT RAIL

Melbourne's excellent public transportation system is centered around its tram and light rail system. Principal services operate from Swanston and Elizabeth streets (north and south); Flinders, Collins and Bourke streets and Batman Avenue (east and west). Trams operate between 5am and midnight Mon–Sat, and 7am and 11pm Sun.

The distinctive burgundy and gold free City Circle Trams run in both directions around the entire city center, at 12-minute intervals, from 10am to 6pm Sun–Wed and from 10am to 9pm Thu–Sat.

## AIRPORT BUS

Skybus runs to Melbourne Airport, around the clock, daily. Drop-offs and pick-ups are available at hotels and at Southern Cross Bus Station. Cost is A$18 for adults and A$25 to A$40 for a family ticket (tel 9600 1711).

## BUSES

Melbourne's buses vary in color, depending on the company. Skybus (tel 9600 1722, skybus. com.au) runs between Melbourne Airport and the city terminus. Privately run hop-on, hop-off buses take passengers around the main sights.

There are no specific bus terminals for suburban buses. Catch them at designated stops. Buy a myki card before you board (see Public Transport panel).

Nightrider Buses can take you home safely between 12.30am and 4.30am on Saturday or Sunday mornings. They head for various suburban destinations and run at hourly intervals, picking up at designated stops, including those close to the major nightlife venues.

## CAR HIRE

Hiring a car may be necessary for some of the out-of-town trips within this book. You must be over 21. Compulsory third-party insurance is included in rental prices, which are on average

A$70–A$90 per day. Overseas visitors require an international driving license.

Major Melbourne car rental companies are: Avis (tel 136 333); Budget (tel 1300 362 848); and Hertz (tel 133 039).

Full details of Australia's road rules are available from the Australian Automobile Association in Canberra (aaa.asn.au).

## FERRIES

Ferries run from Southgate and from World Trade Centre wharves. These are primarily for tours but a ferry runs to Williamstown, from Southbank and St. Kilda, as public transport. Buy tickets directly from the operators.

## TAXIS

Taxis are meter-operated, yellow and conspicuously marked with a "Taxi" sign on top of the vehicle. The basic charge is around A$3.20 (plus a booking fee of A$2) and the remainder of the fare is calculated based on time and distance (from A$1.60 per kilometer).

Main operators include 13 Cabs (tel 132 227) and Silver Top (tel 131 008). Ask for a taxi that can take a wheelchair if you need one.

## TRAINS

Melbourne's inner-city rail lines include the City Loop (Parliament, Melbourne Central, Flagstaff Gardens, Southern Cross Station and Flinders Street Station).

Flinders Street Station is the main suburban rail terminus. Buy a myki card from booths or machines, and enter platforms via the automatic barriers. Trains operate 5am–midnight Mon–Sat, 7am–11pm Sun.

## BICYCLES

Melbourne Bike Share provides locals and tourists with blue bikes and helmets to get around the city's many cycle lanes. There are lots of bike-share stations around the CBD where you can pick up and drop off a bike. Subscribe online at melbournebikeshare.com.au.

### ETIQUETTE

● Smoking is prohibited on public transport (including all internal flights and inside airport terminals), in cinemas, theaters, shops and shopping centers. Some restaurants provide smoking areas.

● There's no mandatory tipping in Melbourne. In restaurants and bars a 10 percent GST (goods and services) tax is included in your bill. However, it is commonplace, and appreciated, to leave a little extra for good waiting service.

### STUDENT TRAVELERS

● International Student Identity Cards are not usually recognized by cinemas, theaters or public transport authorities, but you may be able to get concessions on bus travel.

● There are many backpackers' lodges, YHA establishments and hostels in Melbourne (all busy in summer). YHA cardholders may obtain discounts.

### TRAVEL INSURANCE

Ensure you have the appropriate insurance cover before departure.

# Essential Facts

## OPENING HOURS

● Shops: in the city center generally Mon–Thu 10–6; Fri 10–9; Sat–Sun 10–6. Suburban hours vary; corner shops often open daily 8–8 or later.

● Banks: Mon–Thu 9.30–4; Fri 9.30–5. City head-office banks open Mon–Fri 8.15–5.

● Museums and galleries: generally daily 10–5. Some close on one day of the week and hours may vary from day to day.

● Offices: Mon–Fri 9–5 (5.30 in some cases).

## MONEY

The Australian unit of currency is the Australian dollar (A$), comprising 100 cents. Banknotes come in A$100, A$50, A$20, A$10 and A$5 denominations. Coins come in 5¢, 10¢, 20¢ and 50¢ (silver), and A$1 and A$2 (gold colored).

## ELECTRICITY

● The electricity supply in Australia is 230–250 volts AC. Three-flat-pin plugs are the standard but are not the same as in the UK and adaptors are needed.

● Hotels provide standard 110-volt and 240-volt shaver sockets.

## GOODS & SERVICES TAX (GST)

A 10 percent GST applies to all goods and services. The charge is added to bills.

## INTERNATIONAL NEWSAGENTS

UK and US newspapers, as well as many foreign-language papers, are available from larger newsagents around the city center, including Mitty's News Agency, 53 Bourke Street.

## MAGAZINES

*Beat* magazine (beat.com.au) is Melbourne's gig guide and *Timeout Melbourne* (au.timeout. com/melbourne/) is the city's entertainment guide.

## MEDICAL TREATMENT

● Doctors and dentists are readily available and there are many medical centers where appointments are not necessary.

● Hotels will help you locate a doctor.

● Medical, dental and ambulance services are excellent, but costly.

● British, New Zealand and some other nationals are entitled to "immediate necessary treatment" under a reciprocal agreement but health insurance is still advisable. Dental services are not included.

## MEDICINES

Visitors are permitted to bring prescribed medication in reasonable amounts. Remember to bring your prescription and leave medications in their original containers to avoid problems at customs. Most prescription drugs are widely available here.

## NATIONAL, STATE AND SCHOOL HOLIDAYS
- 1 January: New Year's Day
- 26 January: Australia Day
- 2nd Monday in March: Labour Day (Victorian state holiday)
- Good Friday
- Easter Monday
- 25 April: Anzac Day
- 2nd Monday in June: Queen's Birthday
- 1st Tuesday in November: Melbourne Cup
- 25 December: Christmas Day
- 26 December: Christmas holiday
- School summer holidays are from mid-December to late January—transport, accommodation and tourist facilities are heavily booked at this time.

## NEWSPAPERS
- The main national daily newspaper is *The Australian;* read *The Australian Financial Review* for business news.
- The city's daily newspapers are *The Age*, giving a reasonable coverage of international news, and *The Herald Sun,* a tabloid-style paper published in several editions throughout the day.

## RADIO
Melbourne has many radio stations, ranging from local community stations RRR and PBS, to FM rock music broadcasters such as Triple J-FM and Triple M-FM, to the Australian Broadcasting Corporation's (ABC) Radio National. There are also many AM music, chat and news stations.

## TELEPHONES
- Public telephones are found at phone booths, post offices, hotels, petrol stations, shops, railway and bus stations, and cafés.
- Local calls cost 50¢ for unlimited time.
- Long-distance calls within Australia, known as STD calls, vary in price, but you should have a good supply of 50¢, A$1 and A$2 coins.
- Call 12550 for reverse charge calls.
- Call 1234 for directory assistance.

## TOURIST INFORMATION
- Tourism Victoria
☎ 9653 9777;
tourism.vic.gov.au
- City of Melbourne Visitor Information Centre
✉ Federation Square
☎ 9658 9658;
melbourne.vic.gov.au
🕐 Mon–Fri 7.30–5

**NEED TO KNOW** ESSENTIAL FACTS

## POST OFFICES AND POSTAGE

● Post offices are generally open Mon–Fri 9–5. Melbourne General Post Office hours are Mon–Fri 8.15–5.30, Sat 8.30–noon.
● Larger post offices sell airmails, and provide fax and email facilities.
● Stamps can also be purchased in some hotels and from some newsagents and souvenir shops.

## ADVICE

● If you experience a theft or any other incident, report it to your hotel and the police. If your traveler's checks are stolen, tell the relevant organization.
● It is safe to drink tap water.
● The only medical problems you are likely to experience are sunburn and mosquito bites.
● For sun protection, make sure you wear sun block, sunglasses, a hat and long sleeves if you burn easily.
● Dangerous currents can cause problems in the sea in summer. Swim only at beaches with lifeguards, swim between the flags and observe any posted warnings.
● If you undertake long hikes, let someone know of your expected return time.

● Phonecards come in values of A$5 to A$50; credit cards can be used from some phones.
● International calls, known as ISD calls, can be made from your hotel and certain public telephones by dialing 0011, followed by the country codes: UK 44; US and Canada 1; France 33; Germany 49.
● To call a Melbourne or Victoria number from outside the state, use the prefix 03. Calls from within the state require no prefix.

## TELEVISION

● ABC (Australian Broadcasting Corporation) Channel 2 has no commercials.
● Melbourne has four commercial stations: Channels 7, Nine, Ten and SBS (Special Broadcasting Service). Channel 7 has two sister channels, 7Two and 7Mate. Network Nine's sister channels include Go!, Gem and eXtra. Network Ten's sister station is Channel Eleven. SBS has SBS2, SBS Three and NITV, the National Indigenous Station. Melbourne also has a local community station, Channel 31.
● Cable and satellite services are available in most major hotels.

## TOILETS

There is access to free public toilets in parks, public places, galleries, museums, department stores and also in bus and railway stations.

## VISITORS WITH DISABILITIES

People with mobility related impairments have a number of options for getting around in Melbourne. Many taxis have wheelchair access and the more modern trams and buses have wheelchair access and special seating. There are a number of accessible toilets, which meet current Australian Standards. Many attractions and sporting venues accommodate visitors with mobility related impairments. All parks provide wheelchair accessible paths and some also have accessible toilets. More details can be found on the Visit Melbourne website: visitmelbourne.com under "Information."

# Language

Most people understand the greeting "G'day" as being Australian slang for "hello." But there are lots of other less familiar words and phrases that you might not recognize when talking with the locals. Australians sometimes say several words as one "waddayareckon" ("what do you reckon?") and "owyagoin" ("how are you going?"). This can be confusing, but you will soon get used to it. Listed here are the meanings of some of the words and phrases you're most likely to hear.

## AUSSIE ENGLISH

| | | | |
|---|---|---|---|
| amber fluid | *beer* | larrikin | *lout, mischievous* |
| ankle biter | *small or young child* | lollies | *candy, sweets* |
| | | pommie | *English person* |
| arvo | *afternoon* | rack off | *go away, get lost* |
| barney | *argument, fight* | sanger | *sandwich* |
| big smoke | *the city* | sheila | *girl, woman* |
| bloke | *man* | skite | *boast, brag* |
| bonza | *excellent, attractive* | slab | *carton of 24 beer cans* |
| bush | *the country* | stoked | *very pleased* |
| chinwag | *chat, conversation* | struth! | *exclamation of surprise* |
| cobber | *mate, friend* | stubby | *small bottle of beer* |
| dunny | *outside toilet* | | |
| fair dinkum | *real, genuine, true* | sunnies | *pair of sunglasses* |
| | | tee up | *to organize something* |
| full as a boot | *intoxicated* | | |
| get stuffed | *go away* | tinnie | *can of beer* |
| hard yakka | *hard work* | true blue | *genuine* |
| hooroo | *goodbye* | tucker | *food* |
| knock off | *to steal some-thing, a counter-feit product* | yarn | *story* |
| | | yonks | *long period of time* |

# Timeline

**ASMANIA**

## ABORIGINAL PRESENCE

The Aboriginal people of the Port Phillip area lived in harmony with nature and by their traditional means for thousands of years before European settlement. The nearly 40 different tribal groups throughout present-day Victoria are descendants of people who made their way to the Australian mainland from Southeast Asia up to 60,000 years ago, and led a seminomadic existence. Hunting and gathering for sustenance, the people were bonded to their surroundings by a complex system of spiritual beliefs, and their lives were governed by cultural codes handed down through the generations.

*From left to right: Captain James Cook (1728–79); early Aboriginal people; gold nuggets, panned during the Klondike gold rush; Old Parliament House; Quantas, the national airline of Australia*

### *40,000–60,000 years ago*
Aboriginal people arrive from Southeast Asia.

**1770** English navigator Captain James Cook and the crew of the *Endeavour* arrive in Botany Bay, near the present location of Sydney.

**1787** The First Fleet departs from Portsmouth, England. The 11 ships carry 1,400 people, comprising 756 convicts and a contingent of 644 soldiers.

**1803** The British send ships to Port Phillip Bay to prevent French settlement.

**1835** John Batman buys land around Port Phillip Bay from the Aboriginal people. Two years later, the site is renamed Melbourne, after the British Prime Minister.

**1851** Gold is discovered near Ballarat. People flock from all over the world and Melbourne's population multiplies rapidly. The colony of Victoria separates from New South Wales.

**1860s** As Melbourne prospers, the foundations are laid for many grand buildings.

**1861** The first Melbourne Cup is run.

**1883** The first railway service begins between Melbourne and Sydney.

**1890s** Economic depression ends boom times for the country.

SPIRIT OF TASMANIA

**1901** The Commonwealth of Australia is proclaimed, joining the six Australian colonies into a federation; the first Commonwealth Parliament opens in Melbourne.

**1918** World War I ends. Sixty thousand Australians have died.

**1927** Federal Parliament opens in Canberra.

**1929** The Great Depression begins.

**1939** Black Friday bush fires kill 71 people in Victoria.

**1939–45** Australian troops fight overseas during World War II, with more than 35,000 deaths.

**1956** First television broadcast in Melbourne. The city hosts the XVI Olympiad.

**1994** Native Title Bill becomes law.

**1999** Australia votes against becoming a republic.

**2007** Prime Minister John Howard's 11 years in office comes to an end.

**2010** Julia Gillard becomes Australia's first female prime minister.

**2015** Australia is invited to take part in the Eurovision Song Contest.

### BOOM OR BUST

From the time of the gold rush onwards, and culminating in the Great Exhibition of 1888, the city of Melbourne enjoyed boom times created by the state's enormous mineral wealth. However, the bubble burst in the 1890s and the period of great economic depression that followed ruined numerous speculators and brought great hardship to many.

**NEED TO KNOW** TIMELINE

# Index

# Melbourne 25 Best

**WRITTEN BY** Rod Ritchie
**ADDITIONAL WRITING BY** Julie Walkden
**UPDATED BY** Lou McGregor
**SERIES EDITOR** Clare Ashton
**COVER DESIGN** Chie Ushio, Yuko Inagaki
**DESIGN WORK** Tracey Butler
**IMAGE RETOUCHING AND REPRO** Jacqueline Street-Elkayam

Published in the United Kingdom by AA Publishing

**ISBN 978-1-1018-7946-7**

**FIRST EDITION**

All details in this book are based on information supplied to us at press time. Always confirm information when it matters, especially if you're making a detour to visit a specific place. Fodor's expressly disclaims any liability, loss, or risk, personal or otherwise, that is incurred as a consequence of the use of any of the contents of this book.

**SPECIAL SALES**
This book is available for special discounts for bulk purchases for sales promotions or premiums. For more information, email specialmarkets@randomhouse.com.

Color separation by AA Digital Department
Printed and bound by Leo Paper Products, China

10 9 8 7 6 5 4 3 2 1

A05314
Maps in this title produced from mapping data supplied by Global Mapping, Brackley, UK © Global Mapping
Transport map © Communicarta Ltd, UK

The Automobile Association wishes to thank the following photographers, companies and picture libraries for their assistance in the preparation of this book.

Front cover clockwise from left to right: Alyssand | Dreamstime.com; Filipe Frazao / Shutterstock; InavanHateren / Shutterstock; Neale Cousland / Shutterstock; Greg Brave / Shutterstock; Neale Cousland / Shutterstock; Aleksandar Todorovic / Shutterstock.

2–6bl AA/B Bachman; 6bc AA/J Freeman; 6br Peter Dunphy/Tourism Victoria; 7t AA/B Bachman; 7cl AA/C Sawyer; 7cc Tim Webster/Tourism Victoria; 7cr–7b AA/B Bachman; 7bc–7br Peter Dunphy/Tourism Victoria; 8t–10tcr AA/B Bachman; 10/11 Photodisc; 10br Photodisc; 11t–11tcl AA/B Bachman; 11bl Peter Dunphy/Tourism Victoria; 12–14tcr AA/B Bachman; 14bcr Photodisc; 14br–16t AA/B Bachman; 16tr AA/T Harris; 16tcr 918023305 Tourism Victoria; 16bcr Victor Fraile/Alamy; 16br Peter Dunphy/Tourism Victoria; 17t AA/B Bachman; 17tl Bindi Cole - Snap Happy/ Tourism Victoria; 17tcl Mark Chew/Tourism Victoria; 17bcl AA/C Sawyer; 17bl Melbourne Planetarium, Scienceworks; 18t AA/B Bachman; 18tr Peter Dunphy/Tourism Victoria; 18tcr AA/B Bachman; 18bcr Peter Dunphy/ Tourism Victoria; 18br–19 (ii) AA/B Bachman; 19 (iii) Gavin Hansford/ Tourism Victoria; 19(iv)–(vi) AA/B Bachman; 20/21 Peter Dunphy/Tourism Victoria; 24tl AA/B Bachman; 24tr David Hannah/Tourism Victoria; 25tl Gavin Hansford/Tourism Victoria; 25tr–27tr AA/B Bachman 28tl OMG upstairs National Trust of Australia (Victoria); 28tc–29 National Trust of Australia (Victoria); 30–31t AA/B Bachman 30bl Media Unit - Tourism Victoria; 30br– 33t AA/B Bachman; 34-35t Mark Chew/Tourism Victoria; 36–37t Tourism Victoria; 37c–38t Mark Chew/Tourism Victoria; 39–42l Peter Dunphy/ Tourism Victoria; 42/43t AA/B Bachman; 42/43c Peter Dunphy/Tourism Victoria; 43c Mark Chew/Tourism Victoria; 44tl–44tr Peter Dunphy/Tourism Victoria; 45tl Immigration Museum; 45tr–46/47c AA/B Bachman; 48tl James Lauritz/Tourism Victoria; 48tr Peter Dunphy/Tourism Victoria; 49–50t AA/B Bachman; 50bl Rafael Ben-Ari/Alamy; 50br Enzo Amato/Tourism Victoria; 51t Mark Chew/Tourism Victoria; 51c Tourism Victoria; 52 Mark Chew/ Tourism Victoria; 53–58 Peter Dunphy/Tourism Victoria; 59t AA/A Baker; 59cl–59cr Peter Dunphy/Tourism Victoria; 60l Royal Botanic Gardens; 60/61t AA/B Bachman; 60/61cl AA/J Wood; 61c AA/B Bachman; 61cr Royal Botanic Gardens; 62tl Peter Dunphy/Tourism Victoria; 62tc–64t AA/B Bachman; 65-66t Mark Chew/Tourism Victoria; 67t Tourism Victoria; 68t Mark Chew/ Tourism Victoria; 69 AA/B Bachman; 72 Gavin Hansford/Tourism Victoria; 73tl Tourism Victoria; 73tr AA/A Baker; 74tl David Hannah/Tourism Victoria; 74tr–75b AA/B Bachman; 76 Photodisc; 77t Mark Chew/Tourism Victoria; 77c Tourism Victoria; 78t Mark Chew/Tourism Victoria; 79 AA/B Bachman; 82tl White Studios/Tourism Victoria; 82tr Tim Webster/Tourism Victoria; 83tl– 87 AA/B Bachman; 88 Mark Chew/Tourism Victoria; 89 Tourism Victoria; 90 Mark Chew/Tourism Victoria; 91 AA/B Bachman; 94tl Heide Museum of Modern Art Collection; Commissioned through the Heide Foundation with significant; assistance from Lindsay and Paula Fox 2005; Photographer: John Gollings 2006; © Inge King & John Gollings; 94tr Architect: O'Connor + Houle Architecture; Photographer: John Gollings 2006; © John Gollings; 95tl AA/B Bachman; 95tr National Trust of Australia (Victoria); 96tl–96tr Scienceworks; 97–101/102t AA/B Bachman; 103t Mark Chew/Tourism Victoria; 104 Tourism Victoria; 105 AA/B Bachman; 106 Mark Chew/Tourism Victoria; 107 Peter Dunphy/Tourism Victoria; 108–112t AA/C Sawyer; 108tr–108tcr Stockbyte Royalty Free; 108bcr Mark Chew/Tourism Victoria; 108br AA/B Bachman; 114–125t AA/B Bachman; 123 AA/C Osborne; 124bl AA; 124bc AA; 124br AA/C Coe; 125bl AA/A Baker; 125br AA/M Langford.

Every effort has been made to trace the copyright holders, and we apologize in advance for any unintentional omissions or errors. We would be pleased to apply any corrections in a following edition of this publication.

# Titles in the Series